YOUTH MI

SPCK Library of Ministry

Being a Chaplain
Miranda Threlfall-Holmes and Mark Newitt

Community and Ministry: An introduction to community
development in a Christian context
Paul Ballard and Lesley Husselbee

How to Make Great Appointments in the Church:
Calling, Competence and Chemistry
Claire Pedrick and Su Blanch

Pioneer Ministry and Fresh Expressions of Church
Angela Shier-Jones

Reader Ministry Explored
Cathy Rowling and Paula Gooder

Reflective Caring: Imaginative listening to pastoral experience
Bob Whorton

Skills for Collaborative Ministry
Sally Nash, Jo Pimlott and Paul Nash

Supporting Dying Children and their Families:
A handbook for Christian ministry
Paul Nash

Supporting New Ministers in the Local Church:
A handbook
Keith Lamdin and David Tilley

Tools for Reflective Ministry
Sally Nash and Paul Nash

Youth Ministry: A multi-faceted approach
Sally Nash

YOUTH MINISTRY

A multi-faceted approach

SPCK Library of Ministry

Edited by SALLY NASH

To all students of CYM, past, present and future

First published in Great Britain in 2011

Society for Promoting Christian Knowledge
36 Causton Street
London SW1P 4ST
www.spckpublishing.co.uk

British Library Cataloguing-in-Publication Data
A catalogue record for this book is available from the British Library

ISBN 978-0-281-06342-0
eBook ISBN 978-0-281-06722-0

Typeset by Graphicraft Ltd, Hong Kong
First printed in Great Britain by MPG Books Group
Subsequently digitally printed in Great Britain

Produced on paper from sustainable forests

Contents

Contents

Contributors

Robin Barden is a qualified youth and community worker with over twenty years' experience in a variety of faith-based contexts. Married to Sam, he has lived and worked in and around Cambridge all his life. He has an MA in philosophy and religion from Heythrop College (University of London) and is currently the Assistant Centre Director at the Centre for Youth Ministry (CYM) Cambridge.

Simon Davies has been teaching and training Christian youth workers for seven years with CYM, having previously developed church- and community-based youth work in both Christian and statutory sectors. He volunteers as youth work management team leader in his local church in west Oxfordshire, is married and enjoys film, reading and music.

Jean Harper was previously the Director of London CYM. She remains a keen supporter of lifelong learning and continues to work with students on the CYM courses as a fieldwork tutor as well as being a practice tutor for Oasis College. Until recently Jean was a senior youth worker for a London borough; she is a Girls' Brigade officer and foster carer.

Steve Hirst is a graduate of the Midlands Centre for Youth Ministry (MCYM) and was on placement at Lift Community Trust. After graduating he moved to Ghana and worked with a project for street children and orphans, which he has established as a UK charity – Future Leaders UCC – also setting up a social enterprise offering young people the opportunity to volunteer. His interests involve playing football, going to the gym and being in the outdoors!

The Revd Iain Hoskins is Director of Bristol CYM and enjoys living out his calling to ministry, relishing every minute of it. He believes that there is no greater ministry than the privilege of walking with others in search of a deeper understanding of our creator God. His wife Val is a great support, tolerating his changes of mind and sparks of inspiration – exciting times!

Sharon McKibbin is the Assistant Centre Director in the Centre for Youth Ministry Ireland, having previously worked in a youth homelessness prevention service in Belfast. She has a Master's degree in youth and community work, is JNC professionally qualified and has experience working with young people in different settings, including church-based youth work.

The Revd Dr Bob Mayo is the vicar of St Stephen's, Shepherd's Bush. He co-authored *Making Sense of Generation Y* (Church House Publishing, 2006) and *The Faith of Generation Y* (Church House Publishing, 2010). He is a founder member of the Centre for Youth Ministry and previously Director of Youth and Community Work at Ridley Hall.

The Revd Paul Nash is Senior Chaplain at Birmingham Children's Hospital and a tutor at the Midlands Centre for Youth Ministry. His interests include theological reflection, ethics, ministerial formation and bereavement. He has written *Supporting Dying Children and Their Families* (SPCK, 2011) and co-authored *Skills for Collaborative Ministry* (SPCK, 2008) and *Tools for Reflective Ministry* (SPCK, 2009). To relax he plays golf, and he enjoys coastal walks and holidays in Cornwall.

Dr Sally Nash is Director of the Midlands Centre for Youth Ministry and was part of the group that established the Centre for Youth Ministry in the 1990s. Her involvement in training youth workers began with Youth for Christ in 1984 and her current youth work practice includes working with young people with mental health problems. She has authored and co-authored a number of books and papers on ministry, spirituality and well-being as well as youth work. She is a passionate Spurs supporter and enjoys golf, walking by the sea and research and writing.

Bev Palmer gained her Youth Work degree at MCYM in 2002 and has since worked with young people as a counsellor, spiritual development officer, church youth worker, schools youth worker and latterly as a senior behaviour specialist. She has written articles for *Youthwork* magazine as well as writing and delivering bespoke courses for young people and adults on emotional intelligence.

Sara Reynolds is a qualified youth and community worker who has experience in mentoring, church-based groups and working in schools. She is currently working with Nottingham Youth for Christ and Birmingham Children's Hospital, and is developing her silversmith business.

Dr Sam Richards is Director of Oxford CYM and has been involved in training Christian youth workers for 20 years. She was a youth worker and director of Oxford Youth Works, and has worked mostly with unchurched young people in long-term relational work. She trained with the Clinical Theology Association and Centre 33 young people's counselling service, and has been involved in pastoral care and counselling. She is part of mayBe community, an emerging church project in Oxford. Sam is married to Dave, a professional classic car nut, and they have one young daughter, Ariane. Sam enjoys exploring the world, playing with Ariane and eating chocolate.

Dr Nick Shepherd is CEO and Team Leader for CYM. Nick has been involved in youth ministry since the 1990s and directed the work of Youth for Christ in Bath and Greenwich. Nick holds a PhD from King's College London, where he undertook research into young people's participation in Christian youth work. He is an active member of his local Anglican parish church, supporting the youth ministry there and serving as a Reader.

Jo Whitehead is Assistant Director of the Midlands Centre for Youth Ministry, based at St John's College, Nottingham. She has co-authored a range of books including *Youthwork after Christendom* (Paternoster, 2008) and *Skills for Collaborative Ministry* (SPCK, 2008). She acts as editor for the Grove Youth Series of booklets. She is passionate about training, communicating and writing and loves gardening, walking and all kinds of creative projects.

For further information about CYM, see <www.centreforyouthministry. ac.uk>.

Preface

We must view young people not as empty bottles to be filled but as candles to be lit. (Robert Shaffer)

Many candles can be kindled from one candle without diminishing it. (The Midrash)

You're here to be light, bringing out the God-colors in the world. God is not a secret to be kept. (Matthew 5.15, *The Message*)

Light is often used as a metaphor and our hope is that this book offers light to those who work with young people. This book represents over two hundred years of practical wisdom and experience from staff and students, former and present, of the Centre for Youth Ministry (CYM, <www.centreforyouthministry.ac.uk>). It offers a range of metaphors as a lens through which to understand the different facets of youth ministry. CYM has a philosophy of partnership with individuals and organizations working together to create courses with a Christian value base to equip people to work effectively, professionally and passionately with young people. CYM also now offers courses for those wanting to work with children and families, in schools and in pioneer contexts.

The chapter titles are mine and emerged over a period of time, in many ways, over the 35 years that I have been involved in work with young people. I deliberately chose metaphors as I am convinced by their value: 'The strength of metaphor lies in its potential to assist change through reflection on one's own practices' (Mackinnon 2004: 404). I am delighted at the way that these metaphors have been developed and explored and the resulting book is so much richer than if I had written it myself. I am very grateful for all the contributors who carved time out of busy lives to share of themselves and their experiences. I hope that just as the book has been written by a team, so it can be read with team in mind or by teams. There are 12 roles or facets or dimensions of youth ministry offered, and while we may have to do bits of all of them at times there will clearly be areas where we feel a stronger sense of calling and gifting than others (the Appendix may help clarify this). This is where teams are so valuable: we can work together and the whole is somehow much bigger than the individual parts. Paul puts it very clearly in his letter to the church at Rome:

> In this way we are like the various parts of a human body. Each part gets its meaning from the body as a whole, not the other way around. The body we're talking about is Christ's body of chosen people. Each of us finds our meaning and function as a part of his body. But as a chopped-off finger or cut-off toe we wouldn't amount to much, would we? So since we find ourselves fashioned into all these excellently formed and marvelously functioning parts in Christ's body, let's just go ahead and be what we were made to be, without enviously or pridefully comparing ourselves with each other, or trying to be something we aren't.   (Romans 12.4–6, *The Message*)

My hope is that this book encourages those involved in youth ministry as volunteers, employed workers or managers to explore what they do and perhaps be able to articulate more clearly the nature of the work and to see where there may be gaps or scope for development.

Sally Nash

References

Mackinnon, J., 2004. 'Academic supervision: seeking metaphors and models for quality', *Journal of Further and Higher Education* 28(4): 395–405.
Peterson, E., 2002. *The Message.* Colorado Springs, NavPress.

Introduction

SALLY NASH

[Jesus said] I came so they can have real and eternal life, more and better life than they ever dreamed of.   (John 10.10, *The Message*)

'. . . nobody talks about love. That's all dead.' This half-headline in the *Sunday Times* (Walter 2010) caught my eye. It was for an article about the lives of young women today – so different from my own experience and a very different perspective on liberation. The next morning the first ever song played by Chris Evans on his new breakfast show on Radio 2 was the Beatles' 'All you need is love'. I was struck by this choice and the difference with the article I had read the day before, and couldn't help lamenting lives lacking in love. My thoughts then turned to my teaching for the term – a module on human development where much of what I was reading stressed the importance of loving relationships in our lives. I started wondering what the implications were for those of us who talk about a God of love, and how yet again we may need to revisit the way we try to communicate the gospel to young people.

Such cultural changes and challenges are why this is not simply a how-to-do-youth-ministry book. Rather, it offers a philosophy of youth ministry and an exploration of some of the roles that youth workers play. The hope is that you will be inspired and encouraged and want to contextualize the approaches we are talking about into your own situation. Youth ministry is multifaceted, it is not a one-dimensional activity; it is about facilitating and empowering young people to have the better, fuller, more abundant, rich and satisfying life that different translations of John 10.10 talk about. This involves being concerned about their whole lives, not just the faith bit, wanting to see them fulfil their potential and be all God created them to be. There are plenty of resources that offer ideas and content for youth work sessions: *Youthwork* magazine, Youth for Christ, Scripture Union, CPAS, Urban Saints and many others offer such resources, and a visit to your local Christian bookshop will enable you to browse through what is out there – sometimes more useful than buying something online and finding it is not what you had hoped!

Young people today

As I am writing this introduction David Cameron is announcing a £2 million quest to measure the quality of life for British people, phrased as 'happiness' or 'well-being'. I have elsewhere encouraged an approach to youth work that seeks to enhance the well-being of young people (Nash and Pimlott 2010). A look at recent news reports about young people shows that there is a cause for concern. A review of one week in November 2010 highlights these issues:

- Young people are twice as likely to be living on disability benefits in the UK as they are in other rich countries, says OECD.
- Young people with mental illness and learning difficulties are being let down by the youth justice system, a new report reveals.
- One-fifth of 18-year-olds are officially not in education, employment or training.

(Source: <www.guardian.co.uk/society/youngpeople>)

A range of recent reports also highlight a lack of well-being for young people in the UK with, for example, the Child Poverty Action Group (2009: 2) ranking the UK twenty-fourth out of 29 in child well-being and poverty in Europe. However, following on from their *Good Childhood Enquiry* (2009), the Children's Society have developed a project to understand the well-being of children and young people from their own perspective and the results of this study are more encouraging. The Society studied just under 7,000 10–15-year-olds and summarized their findings thus:

> The general picture is that most young people surveyed were faring well – the average well-being score was 7.7 on a scale from 0 to 10. But a minority – in the region of 7 to 10 per cent – could be said to be 'unhappy' or to have 'low well-being'. (Children's Society 2010: 3)

Thus this report, which actually asked young people what they thought, gives us more hope as to the state of young people in the UK today.

The New Economics Foundation defines well-being as:

- people's satisfaction with their life, including satisfaction, pleasure and enjoyment;
- people's personal development, including being engaged in life, curiosity, 'flow' (a state of absorption where hours pass like minutes), personal development and growth, autonomy, fulfilling potential, having a purpose in life and the feeling that life has meaning;
- people's social well-being – a sense of belonging to our communities, a positive attitude towards others, feeling that we are contributing to society and engaging in pro-social behaviour, and believing that society is capable of developing positively.

(Shah and Marks 2004: 2)

Reading this definition, it is clear that youth work has much to offer in enhancing the well-being of young people. This book reflects such an emphasis and has a strong focus on ways of working with young people one-to-one as well as in groups; chapters on self-esteem, pastoral care, spiritual development and being a guide to young people offer ideas, skills and suggestions which should be particularly useful, and other chapters emphasize building and developing young people in a group and community context.

Shalom

In the Christian context, well-being can be framed in terms of shalom. Ingram suggests that shalom as well-being 'probably underlies all its other uses in some way or other' (2008: 3). He suggests that well-being in the Old Testament encompasses living well in all areas of life, and helpfully illustrates how shalom is echoed in the five outcomes of 'Every Child Matters', a core policy for work with children and young people (in the English context):

- Be healthy, e.g. Psalm 38.3, 'There is no soundness in my flesh because of your indignation; there is no health [shalom] in my bones because of my sin.'
- Stay safe, e.g. 1 Samuel 20.21, 'If I say to the boy, "Look, the arrows are on this side of you, collect them", then you are to come, for, as the LORD lives, it is safe [shalom] for you and there is no danger.'
- Enjoy and achieve, e.g. Isaiah 55.12, 'For you shall go out in joy, and be led back in peace [shalom]'; Jeremiah 29.11, 'For surely I

know the plans I have for you, says the LORD, plans for your welfare [shalom] and not for harm, to give you a future with hope.'

- Make a positive contribution, e.g. Jeremiah 29.7, 'But seek the welfare [shalom] of the city where I have sent you into exile, and pray to the LORD on its behalf, for in its welfare [shalom] you will find your welfare [shalom].'
- Achieve economic well-being, e.g. Psalm 37.11, 'But the meek shall inherit the land, and delight in abundant prosperity [shalom].'

(Ingram 2008: 3)

This gives us a way of understanding how biblical principles complement government approaches to work with young people, and how they give us the opportunity to articulate the work we do from a theological perspective while drawing on widely accepted good practice.

Youth ministry today

We are not doing youth ministry in an easy context. 'Compared to previous generations, Generation Y young people are less likely to identify themselves as Christian, less likely to go to church, less likely to hold traditional Christian beliefs' (Collins-Mayo *et al.* 2010: 84). There may be many reasons for this, including changing practices and values among parents and their attitude to Christianity and social changes which mean that there are a lot of competing demands on young people's time, as well as the capacity of the Church to resource its work with young people. Young people's world views are changing; Savage *et al.* (2006) talk about a 'happy midi-narrative', and a significant study in the United States uses the term 'moralistic therapeutic deism' (Smith with Denton 2005). Such world views can lead to young people only accessing faith if and when they think they need it. Mason, talking about the Australian context, comments that 'young people's personal identity now rests on the fragile foundations of family or origin, friendship networks and unstable sexual partnerships, no longer sustained by the massive support of church, neighbourhood and voluntary associations' (2010: 61). The role of the youth worker or minister in both church and missional contexts is vital in continuing to offer a vision of what Christian life looks like lived out with commitment, passion, joy and faithfulness.

If we look at statistics relating to numbers of young people attending church on your average Sunday it is not an encouraging read, with around 6 per cent of 11–14s and 5 per cent of 15–19s there (Brierley 2006), although around 27 per cent of 18–24-year-olds say they belong to the Christian religion (NCSR 2008). Research suggests that young people have a benign indifference to the Church today (Collins-Mayo *et al.* 2010), not the hostility that has sometimes been experienced from previous generations. However, there is a concern about transmission of the Christian faith and ways this might be improved (Collins-Mayo *et al.* 2010; Dean 2010; Shepherd 2010). Although writing from an American context where young people are more churched, Kenda Creasy Dean's experiences resonate with my research and experience:

> We have known for some time that youth groups do important things for teenagers, providing moral formation, learned competencies and social and organizational ties. But they seem less effective as catalysts for consequential faith, which is far more likely to take root in the rich relational soil of families, congregations, and mentor relationships where young people can see what faithful lives look like, and encounter the people who love them enacting a larger story of divine care and hope.
> (Dean 2010: 11)

The hope is that this book will help us to be effective catalysts, and the emphasis on working with individual young people that comes through in several of the chapters underpins our belief that young people need supportive and encouraging relationships with a variety of adults. Thus chapters such as 'Mediating mirror' (Chapter 8), 'Guardian of souls' (Chapter 9), 'Odyssey guide' (Chapter 10) and 'Compassionate presence' (Chapter 11) may be relevant to a wide variety of those who have contact with young people.

It is impossible to give an overview of youth ministry today as it happens in so many diverse places: churches, schools, local projects, national organizations' programmes, for example. Thinking back to my adolescence, I was involved with a church youth group, an independent Crusader group (now Urban Saints) and the Young Sowers' League, as well as the school Christian Union. Looking back now, I think I learnt about mission from church, worship and the Bible from Crusaders, the Bible from the Young Sowers' League and the importance of peer support from the Christian Union. Young people today may have a similar experience, but perhaps with more contemporary-sounding group names! Readers of this book might be doing youth ministry in any or more of these contexts and with a variety of value bases. These are some you may be familiar with:

- mission-oriented (Sudworth 2007) or community ministry (Morisy 1997);
- relationally oriented (Ward 1998; Root 2008);
- theological perspectives, such as practising passion (Dean 2004);
- church-oriented, such as inclusive congregational (integrating young people into congregational life), preparatory (young people as disciples in training with an orientation towards service – present and future), church or congregation planting (Senter 2001);
- spiritual practice-oriented, such as contemplative youth ministry (Yaconelli 2006);
- family-based (DeVries 2004; Gardner 2008);
- value-oriented, such as purpose-driven (Fields 1998);
- culturally informed (Savage *et al.* 2006; Pimlott and Pimlott 2008; Collins-Mayo *et al.* 2010).

This book seeks to equip you to undertake a range of roles within whatever sort of youth ministry you are doing, helping you to become more effective in your work. We are describing a multifaceted youth ministry which we see as encompassing values of being God-focused, inclusive, liberative, restorative, redemptive, empowering, reconciling and incarnational.

Reflecting on your practice

The Centre for Youth Ministry (CYM) seeks to develop reflective practitioners and we would encourage such an approach to this book, exploring how it relates to your context and ministry. We have developed resources to help you do this (Nash 2007; Nash and Nash 2009) but this is a brief introduction. Reflection is a core skill for youth workers and involves 'giving something appropriate attention and consideration, looking at it from a variety of perspectives, being aware of the lenses we use, and making a response' (Nash and Nash 2009: 3). It can be helpful to have a structure to reflect with, to make sure that we have covered the significant areas. This is a basic model that we use which synthesizes a variety of approaches:

1 *Name* What is the situation/issue/dilemma/problem/question?
2 *Explore* What do we hope will emerge from this reflective practice process? What is the end result/product/consequence . . . that we are looking for?
3 *Analyse* What is/could be going on? Have we made any assumptions or presuppositions? How do we/others think/feel? What would our values, motives, goals, agenda, purpose, tradition, discipline want to say? What theory or previous experience informs this? Here also add faith, the Bible, theology, Christian tradition and culture as tools for analysis.
4 *Evaluate* What were/are our options? What would we change/ do differently? What are the possibilities? What are the strengths and weaknesses of these? Why did we come to this conclusion/do this . . . ? Again, you can draw in faith resources at this stage.
5 *Outcome* What is the outcome of this process? New learning/different practice/action/insight . . . (Nash *et al.* 2008: 50).

A quick three-part approach is the idea that we observe, then assess and finally respond (Nash 2007).

As Christians we will want to theologically reflect, which is why at Step 3 we encourage the use of faith-based resources. Theological reflection leads us to ask two key questions:

1 What within my faith resources helps me make sense of, critique, go deeper into or look differently at this situation?
2 Where can I see God and the kingdom in this experience?

A helpful definition is that of Killen and de Beer: 'Theological reflection is the discipline of exploring individual and corporate experience with the wisdom of a religious heritage . . . The outcome is new truth and meaning for living' (1999: viii). You will get more from this book if you theologically reflect on it and seek to contextualize and apply it to your own situation.

The rest of the book

Paul Nash and Steve Hirst introduce us to the idea of a politician of integrity being foundational to youth ministry. They explore how to be a youth worker with integrity. Containing challenging questions and practical examples, this chapter provides a foundation to the rest of the book in considering the character of the youth minister.

Jo Whitehead helps us to see how we can lead through being inspired and encouraged by biblical examples and ultimately by Christ. She emphasizes the importance of authenticity and being who we are, and reminds us to consider how we use power as leaders.

Simon Davies offers an approach to being a visionary architect based on taking us through a step-by-step process of building our youth work. He roots this within a case study and shows how the processes can work themselves out in reality.

Nick Shepherd talks about the importance of community building for young people and challenges us to consider how our youth work is hospitable, honest and humble. His chapter is rooted in his own research and experience, and encourages us to put community building at the heart of Christian youth work and mission.

Bob Mayo argues that the empowering liberator is involved in the task of character formation based on the assumption that character determines choices, and that the beliefs, traditions and values of a person's community shape his or her character. The informal educator is thus involved in helping young people to become the person they want to be. This offers a liberating approach to what others may call discipleship or mentoring.

Jean Harper explores the importance of the youth worker as party planner, including young people in the planning and delivery of celebrations that help demonstrate a loving, creative God who rejoices in us having fun. She also considers programme planning for our regular activities.

Sharon McKibbin describes the role of the boundary marker. In a practical chapter full of helpful theory and insights, she offers practical wisdom as to how to facilitate groups and respond to challenging behaviour, reminding us that the disciples presented in this way too!

Sam Richards explores self-image and self-esteem in 'Mediating mirror'. She roots her understanding of this role in our identity as Christians and offers some helpful, practical strategies and approaches to enable us to try to mediate a positive identity to the young people we work with.

Jo Whitehead and Sara Reynolds reflect on our role as guardian of souls. They offer an understanding of spiritual and faith development rooted in both theory and their own youth work experiences. They stress the need for strong relationships, but in a context where young people are free to express who they are and where they are on their journey, including doubts and struggles as well as joys and blessings.

Bev Palmer and I take the idea of an odyssey guide and explore how youth workers can get alongside young people and help them in their journeys. We explore what skills and practices are needed, and integrated throughout are the stories of young people. There is also a challenge to be on a journey ourselves in order to be able to help others on their journey.

Robin Barden offers an in-depth analysis of the parable of the Good Samaritan as the root of understanding what it means to be a compassionate presence seeking to offer pastoral care to young people. He identifies important attitudes that we need to adopt in this context and discusses the concept within an understanding of the kingdom of God.

Iain Hoskins discusses self-care and suggests that, as youth workers, many of us find it easy to give care but hard to receive it. He emphasizes the importance of a reciprocal approach to care and suggests some strategies to help us care for ourselves more effectively.

Each chapter has recommendations for further reading – these are the books with a short explanation after them to help you identify which might be relevant. There are also reflection questions that you can use individually or in groups. There is inevitably some cross-fertilization between the chapters, as there are skills, knowledge and understanding that is useful in more than one context and roles are not discrete. Thus material on working one-to-one with young people can be found in several chapters, and there are recurring theological themes such as recognizing that young people are made in the image of God (Genesis 1.27) and that they should be invited to experience life in all its fullness (John 10.10).

The Appendix contains what I have called a 'Youth ministry role preferences and passions indicator', which asks you to consider five statements for each role/metaphor, total the score and then rank the 12 roles. You can use this information to reflect on your preferences and passions and consider areas for development both individually and as part of a team.

Our hope in writing this book is that you will be re-envisioned in your youth work and will reflect on the many roles and facets that can help us attain our goal of building the kingdom of God among young people. The most apt conclusion to this introduction for me is this prayer:

> I pray that, according to the riches of his glory, he may grant that you may be strengthened in your inner being with power through his Spirit, and that Christ may dwell in your hearts through faith, as you are being rooted and grounded in love. I pray that you may have the power to comprehend, with all the saints, what is the breadth and length and height and depth, and to know the love of Christ that surpasses knowledge, so that you may be filled with all the fullness of God.
>
> Now to him who by the power at work within us is able to accomplish abundantly far more than all we can ask or imagine, to him be glory in the church and in Christ Jesus to all generations, for ever and ever. Amen. (Ephesians 3.16–21)

References

Brierley, P., 2006. *Pulling out of the Nosedive: A contemporary portrait of churchgoing – what the 2005 English Church Census reveals*. London, Christian Research.

Child Poverty Action Group, 2009. *Child Wellbeing and Child Poverty: Briefing paper*. London, CPAG.

Children's Society, 2009. *The Good Childhood Enquiry*. London, Children's Society.

Children's Society, 2010. *Understanding Children's Well-being Report Summary*. London, Children's Society.

Collins-Mayo, S., Mayo, B., Nash, S. and Cocksworth, C., 2010. *The Faith of Generation Y*. London, Church House Publishing.

Dean, K. C., 2004. *Practicing Passion*. Grand Rapids, MI, Eerdmans.

Dean, K. C., 2010. *Almost Christian: What the faith of our teenagers is telling the American church*. Oxford, Oxford University Press.

DeVries, M., 2004. *Family Based Youth Ministry*. Chicago, IVP.

Fields, D., 1998. *Purpose-driven Youth Ministry*. Grand Rapids, MI, Zondervan.

Gardner, J., 2008. *Mend the Gap: Can the Church reconnect the generations?* Nottingham, IVP.

Ingram, D., 2008. 'Shalom: Peace . . . or is it?', conference paper presented to Diocesan Directors of Education, Warwick, 10 June.

Killen, P. O. and de Beer, J., 1999. *The Art of Theological Reflection*. New York, Crossroad.

Mason, M., 2010. 'The spirituality of young Australians', in S. Collins-Mayo and P. Dandelion (eds) *Religion and Youth*. Farnham, Ashgate.

Morisy, A., 1997. *Beyond the Good Samaritan*. London, Continuum.

Nash, P., 2007. *What Theology for Youth Work?* London, SPCK.

Nash, S. and Nash, P., 2009. *Tools for Reflective Ministry*. London, SPCK.

Nash, S. and Pimlott, N., 2010. *Well-being and Spirituality*. Cambridge, Grove.

Nash, S., Pimlott, J. and Nash, P., 2008. *Skills for Collaborative Ministry*. London, SPCK.

National Centre for Social Research (NCSR), 2008. *British Social Attitudes Survey*. Colchester, NCSR.

Pimlott, J. and Pimlott, N., 2008. *Youthwork after Christendom*. Carlisle, Paternoster.

Root, A., 2008. *Revisiting Relational Youth Ministry*. Chicago, IVP.

Savage, S., Collins-Mayo, S., Mayo, B. and Cray, G., 2006. *Making Sense of Generation Y*. London: Church House Publishing.

Senter, M. H. (ed.), 2001. *Four Views of Youth Ministry and the Church*. Grand Rapids, MI, Zondervan.

Shah, H. and Marks, N., 2004. *A Well-being Manifesto for a Flourishing Society*. London, NEF.

Shepherd, N. M., 2010. 'Christian youth groups as sites for identity work', in S. Collins-Mayo and P. Dandelion (eds) *Religion and Youth*. Farnham, Ashgate.

Smith, C. with Denton, M. L., 2005. *Soul Searching: The religious and spiritual life of American teenagers*. Oxford, Oxford University Press.

Sudworth, T., 2007. *Mission-shaped Youth: Rethinking young people and church*. London, Church House Publishing.

Walter, N., 2010. 'Pretty baby', *Sunday Times*, 10 January.

Ward, P., 1998. *Youthwork and the Mission of God*. London, SPCK.

Yaconelli, M., 2006. *Contemplative Youth Ministry*. London, SPCK.

1

Politician of integrity

PAUL NASH WITH STEVE HIRST

I never did, or countenanced, in public life, a single act inconsistent with the strictest good faith; having never believed there was one code of morality for a public, and another for a private man.

(Thomas Jefferson, third president of
the United States of America)

It's a good thing to assume, to act on the basis that . . . others are [people] of integrity and honour . . . because you tend to attract integrity and honour if that is how you regard those with whom you work. (Nelson Mandela)

Have you ever asked yourself or been asked by others any of these questions?

- If you were offered your heart's desire, what would it be?
- If you were offered any spiritual gift or character quality, what would it be? If you had to give something up for it, what would you be willing to give up for it?
- Does character matter?

Your answers will reflect something of your approach to integrity.

1

Why do we have a chapter called 'Politician of integrity' in a youth ministry book? Because whenever we work for an organization and with people there are political dimensions. This is politics with a small 'p' which includes things like structural issues, organizational dynamics and power. Integrity is the quality of being honest and having strong moral principles, the state of being whole and undivided, being sound in construction and having internal consistency (all elements from dictionary definitions of 'integrity').

We want to suggest a model of youth worker that picks up the best of being political. Someone who

- represents everyone (John 3.16);
- advocates for marginalized and oppressed groups (Luke 4.18f.);
- has influence and is willing to help (John 11.3);
- treats everyone fairly and with respect (Micah 6.8);
- is trustworthy (1 John 5.14);
- is servant-hearted, wanting the best for those in his or her care (John 13.15–17).

The best politician is a leader of integrity. You know when you have been around people of integrity. It feels different; it feels honest, open, transparent, and fair. They tend to be people who know how to relate to others to bring about the best outcome, and they are able to get things done.

Integrity as a virtue

The concept of a politician of integrity draws on virtue ethics, which is a slightly different way of looking at how we act in our day-to-day life as well as in difficult dilemmas. Virtue ethics has its root in classical thought: Aristotle, Socrates and Plato all wrote about virtue, with Aristotelian ethics being known as virtue theory (Vardy and Grosch 1999). Classic virtues are wisdom, courage, temperance and justice. Virtues are concerned with inner values and the external expressions of those values. For instance, I want to be an honest youth worker, therefore I will be truthful when I am asked how the work is going. Within Christianity the most frequently mentioned virtues are faith, hope and love or charity (1 Corinthians 13.13). As we may well have experienced, to be faithful or loving requires a sustained commitment to act in such a way. We will only become politicians of integrity with repeated choices that reinforce that.

Virtues for Christian youth workers

There are many virtues Christian youth workers can choose to embody and embrace, such as being loving, holy, gracious, forgiving, courageous, respectful, just, wise, humble, honourable, compassionate, equitable, trustworthy, honest, thorough, good. Virtues for caring professions have been identified, such as professional wisdom, care, respectfulness, trustworthiness, justice, courage and integrity (Banks and Gallagher 2009). All these have merit, but if we could have only one what would it be and how would we nurture this choice? The Bible tells us that love is the greatest virtue (1 Corinthians 13.13) but I want to suggest that integrity can make a claim to be the most important virtue in the life of a youth worker: without it everything else may come to nothing.

Case study: fundraising

In organizations Steve has been involved in there have often been ethical debates around the issue of funding, especially funding from government agencies, which may specify that they will not fund religious projects. This raises the question of whether it is ethically wrong for an organization with underlying Christian principles to apply for such funding (even if their work is in no way overtly Christian).

> For me this brings up huge questions about one's definition of 'Christian work' and where one's virtues and principles are birthed. However, within all these questions there is undoubtedly an element of honesty and integrity which must be considered. Within my work we have always considered this and made funding application decisions based on the principles of integrity and of not misleading people. If we have felt that we can maintain these principles and that they are not being compromised then we will happily consider funding from a range of sources.

Definition of a politician of integrity

Our definition of a politician of integrity in a youth work context is

> a virtuous person who, both in public and in private, speaks
> and acts with integrity, displays a commitment to and
> engagement with the work of the kingdom of God (Matthew

6.33) and seeks to have the mind of Christ (1 Corinthians 2.16) and to live a life worthy of his or her calling (Ephesians 4.1), manifesting the fruit of the Spirit (Galatians 5.22).

How can we develop this life of integrity?

To be a politician of integrity is choosing a way of being that encompasses the following qualities, values and virtues:

- graciousness – being generous, gentle, forgiving;
- honesty – not misleading people and speaking the truth in love;
- wisdom – an underrated virtue. We need wisdom before most virtues and need to be wise before we act. Wisdom will save us from much grief and give us a firm foundation for our work;
- bravery – politicians sometimes need to be brave, to make the best decision although they know it will not be immediately popular or perhaps understood;
- shrewdness – what did Jesus mean when he told us to be as wise as serpents and as gentle as doves (Matthew 10.6)? We cannot be naive, thinking others are always honest when they tell us things, ask for our help or offer to help (Luke 16.1–16). I do not tell everyone I meet all that I am thinking all the time. I have a responsibility to be discerning and discreet;
- discernment or good judgement – particularly taking note of the movement of the Holy Spirit within us and our values and principles;
- far-sightedness – articulating what you believe God is doing or is calling you to;
- a servantlike attitude – imitating Jesus, being a servant to all and choosing the lowly position, e.g. clearing up when no one is watching;
- trustworthiness – being a person of your word, doing things for deadlines and being ready for both important and seemingly unimportant meetings;
- advocacy – speaking and acting on behalf of the voiceless, marginalized or oppressed.

To be transparent is to be see-through. One of the criticisms of our politicians is that they act in secret. Now there is nothing wrong with being discreet, and above I commend shrewdness, but our actions and our motivations should be out in the open. Translucence – being semi-transparent – is not good enough. What are your responses if asked by your church leader or young people about films you have seen, websites you have visited, things you have said about other people, how you got so and so to do something for you, how you raised that pot of money. Double test: one of the nicest things that has ever been said to me by a young person was that he had never heard me say anything nasty about someone else, but the double test is what he would have heard me say when I was with my friends or if he could read my thoughts!

Attitudes of a politician of integrity

Decide not to play games. I don't mean football or cricket, I mean colluding with others to manipulate the outcome. Not playing games means taking things seriously, dealing with the real issue and not being side-tracked or taken down a dead end. This can be initiated by us or by others, when they seek to draw us in to rescue or save them, again! Think and act win:win (Covey 2004). To have integrity is to want everyone to win as far as this is possible. Work collaboratively (Nash *et al.* 2008), as to be a leader of integrity will lead us to a place of realizing we cannot do it on our own. This is not because we are not clever or godly enough: it is because we were made to work together (Genesis 1.27). Valuing availability and accountability over ability is important. Steve tells how through his youth work practice he has experienced the truth of that statement:

> At an early stage of a mentoring relationship I remember feeling that this young person's needs were far beyond my level of training, understanding and experience, as he had some very deep-rooted issues. However, through building up a relationship built on accountability and the young person understanding my level of availability I was able to guide him through many of the issues he was facing. It also enabled me to refer him for more specialized support in specific areas.

Self-awareness

Self-awareness is a core skill that is vital for a politician of integrity. As youth workers we must be aware of many things: the needs of our young people, the aspirations of their parents, the principles of the kingdom of God. An underpinning skill to all these is self-awareness. To know myself, my weaknesses, my strengths, my biases, to be aware of all these and more, will enable me to be more effective and to be aware of their consequences in my work. Whether or not we like it – and, as an important aside, I hope not much – we have power and authority. Being aware that we have this is the first step, and learning to handle it healthily and responsibly is the next. Young people, other leaders and adults will look to us to act appropriately and with integrity, and in a way that is not abusive or oppressive. Steve writes,

> I am continuously learning the importance of self-awareness. Through my experiences I am aware this is not only about understanding my own strengths and limitations (which is vital), but also to have an awareness of how my upbringing, world view, class, etc., has impacted who I am and how this is viewed by the people I am working with. For example, for me it is very important to have an understanding of how being a white middle-class man is viewed within the culture that I am working with and how this impacts my interactions. Along with self-awareness it is important to have good self-esteem. If we do not first healthily love ourselves, because God loves us for who we are and not what we can do for him and others, we will be tempted to look for our affirmation from other sources. Loving myself is not an option for an effective ministry, it is essential. If we do not have a healthy God-rooted positive view of ourselves we will have problems exercising integrity, because we will be tempted to look for affirmation, attention, love, inappropriately from others. This is not the path to being a leader of integrity.

Ethical principles

When asked how Jesus taught us to treat each other, a child replied, 'Do unto others before they do it to you.' It's funny partly because we see the truth in it. We encounter other such ethical principles: lying, cheating, stealing, etc., are all right as long as you don't get caught; what I do in private is my own business and none of yours; I can do what I want as long as I don't hurt anyone. We could live our lives like this but it wouldn't be a very nice world. As well as virtue ethics, already mentioned, there are at least two other main ways of making ethical decisions. One is about rules and duty, 'the right thing to do': this is described as deontological. The other is concerned with the outcome, the consequences of something, in some instances the greatest good for the greatest number (utilitarianism): this is sometimes described as teleological. We are all likely to have a default ethical preference, and it can be helpful when reflecting on being a politician of integrity to recognize what this is. Two or three people all acting with integrity according to their own world view could come to very different decisions based on their preferred ethical principles or approach. However, it is difficult to talk about ethics and ethical principles without being aware of cultural factors and the need to take account of the culture (relevance) and to be counter-cultural. It may be helpful to articulate some ethical principles that we work by. The National Youth Agency (2004) has some for professional youth and community work and CYMA, a New Zealand organization, has helpful guidelines for devising your own code (2003/2011).

Whatever model of Christian ethics we embrace or are influenced by, as youth workers we need to both adopt and be shaped by cultural values, and also to speak out and act in an opposite way where appropriate. This is a matter of discernment. For instance, should we adopt the language (swearing) of those staff and young people we work with (cultural) or should we make an effort to ensure our speech reflects what we understand to be biblical standards (counter-cultural)? Steve writes:

A great deal of my experience of youth work has been working within contexts and cultures that are very different from my upbringing and world view: for example, working within inner-city council estates and in street settings in Africa. I have learnt to adopt certain cultural practices and values, but within this I still have to maintain my underlying personal ethics. This creates a very interesting dynamic and tension, which is something I am constantly analysing and reflecting upon. An example of this would be the role of children within my work in Africa. Within that context the cultural belief is that children should contribute significantly within the house, including cleaning, washing and cooking for a number of hours every day. My values and principles are that children should have the opportunity to be children; to play, to have fun, to obtain an education, to interact with friends, etc. It is important that I maintain and don't deny my ethical understanding; however, I must also be open and adaptable to their world view. I have found opportunities where I can implement examples of the importance of play and recreation through my work, without causing offence and still reinforcing the importance of the role of children within their cultural setting. It is possible for me to maintain my integrity and work within their cultural values.

Life by its very nature is complicated, even when we seek to be this virtuous person making ethical decisions. To live and lead with integrity is not without its tensions and paradoxes. For example, it is not always easy to know when we tip over from being discreet to being secretive or deceitful. Sometimes we need to act appropriately in a situation, but it can feel as though we have double standards.

Tests for the youth worker of integrity

- *Is who we are in secret who we are in public?* When we think about these things, our minds can go to the big things such as politicians' expenses, weapons of mass destruction, inappropriate sexual relationships. But this is only part of the equation. Integrity is also about the smaller things, especially about the little details of our lives, those things that we think only we know about: what we watch on TV, how we spend our time and money, what we think about, why we do what we do.
- *Am I driven or do I minister out of passion?* If you are someone who is driven, someone who can't stop, then it is difficult to have integrity: you will always be tempted to seek meaning, purpose, identity from your work rather than being a person who seeks first to be loved by God and then builds the kingdom.
- *Can I be shrewd without being deceitful or manipulative?*
- *Do I look out for number one first, then maybe the needs of others?*

If we can first answer these honestly, be dissatisfied where the answers do not reflect God's standards and aspirations for our lives, and then set our face towards a higher calling to rise to the challenge of Jesus, 'but *I* say to you . . .' (Matthew 5.44, my italic), then we will be people of integrity.

What can this look like?

A politician of integrity does the right thing, first time, for the right reason; it is not just being clever and positioning oneself in a place of influence. How much of this sounds like you? How much do you really want to be like this? If you were in an election hoping to stand for the Integrity Party, would you be perceived as a person and youth worker of integrity who could become their candidate?

Cloud uses the metaphor of the wake from a boat to encourage us to reflect on what we leave behind or what follows us as we go through life and work (2006: 16).

Conclusion

> You have heard all your life that character counts. You have desired integrity in yourself and in the people with whom you work. You have felt its effects, suffered when it has not been present, and benefited when it has. You know that it is real.
>
> (Cloud 2006: ix)

We need to decide and to commit ourselves to the ethical standards we discern as reflecting the values and principles of the kingdom of God and what God requires his ministers to be like. Integrity is imitating the character of God. Being a politician of integrity will not guarantee you a problem-free time – you may have even more – but they will be the problems God wants you to have. Which way will you set your face?

Questions for reflection

- Self-audit: explore the questions asked in the chapter and articulate what kind of person you want to be. What are your areas for development?
- Cloud talks about building trust through vulnerability (2006: 87). This is a risky business: how can you become vulnerable so as to encourage integrity with those you work alongside?
- How can we exercise more integrity with our young people, their parents, the Church, church leadership, each other?
- Personal commitment: I make a commitment not to manipulate, be in it for myself, be two-faced, break promises, pursue self-interest, play games, do things just to look good, be rude about others behind their backs ... To which of these do you need to commit yourself, and what would you add?

References and further reading

Banks, S. and Gallagher, A., 2009. *Ethics in Professional Life*. Basingstoke, Palgrave Macmillan.

Cloud, H., 2006. *Integrity*. New York, Collins. A business book but full of wise advice.

Covey, S., 2004. *Seven Habits of Highly Effective People*. London, Simon and Schuster. An accessible classic containing much wisdom.

CYMA, 2003/2011. *Writing a Code of Ethics*, <www.youthministry.org.nz/?sid=199>.

Nash, S., Pimlott, J. and Nash, P., 2008. *Skills for Collaborative Ministry*. London, SPCK. Lots of practical advice enabling you to work effectively as part of a team.

National Youth Agency, 2004. *Ethical Conduct in Youth Work*. Leicester, NYA; available at <www.nya.org.uk/dynamic_files/workforce/Ethical%20 Conduct%20in%20Youth%20Work%20%28Reprint%202004%29.pdf>.

Steare, R., 2008. *Ethicability*, second edition. Ashford, Roger Steare Consulting. An interesting book to help you explore ethics.

Vardy, P. and Grosch, P., 1999. *The Puzzle of Ethics*, second edition. London, Fount.

2

Flawed hero

JO WHITEHEAD

> Spiritual leaders are not made by election or appointment . . . nor by
> conferences or synods. Only God can make them . . . Religious position
> can be conferred by bishops and boards, but not spiritual authority,
> which is the prime essential of Christian leadership.
>
> (J. Oswald Sanders)

It continues to amaze me, as I read Scripture, that God chooses
the most unlikely individuals to fulfil leadership roles. Most biblical
leaders would struggle to find acceptance in many of today's churches,
never mind being given responsibility and authority there. God seems
to go out of his way to choose people whose character, circumstances, background, upbringing and/or personal choices might
appear to preclude them from exercising any form of leadership.
Moses is rather a wimp who gets his brother to speak on his behalf,
yet he leads a nation out of slavery. Elijah flees for his life, sinks
into depression and wants to die, yet he has just called fire down
from heaven and continues to exercise powerful prophetic ministry.
Esther is in a harem but becomes queen and goes uninvited before
the king, risking her life to prevent genocide. Rahab is a prostitute
but helps God's people and ends up in the lineage of Christ. Noah

gets so drunk he falls unconscious, yet God chooses him out of all people on earth at the time. David sleeps with a married woman and arranges to have her husband killed, yet he becomes one of Israel's greatest kings. Mary is a teenager from a poor family yet is chosen to give birth to God's Son. Saul is a persecutor of the early Church, approving of the stoning of Stephen, yet God chooses him to exercise apostolic missional leadership.

We can only conclude that God has a different perspective on leadership from most of us. Paul himself emphasizes this when he writes to the young church in Corinth:

> Consider your own call, brothers and sisters: not many of you were wise by human standards, not many were powerful, not many were of noble birth. But God chose what is foolish in the world to shame the wise; God chose what is weak in the world to shame the strong; God chose what is low and despised in the world, things that are not, to reduce to nothing things that are, so that no one might boast in the presence of God. (1 Corinthians 1.26–29)

Looking at the great 'heroes' of the Christian faith, then, it is clear that we are exploring a different kind of heroism from that which we might commonly understand. Heroes traditionally are the central characters in stories, often undertaking some kind of quest or challenge and usually displaying either uncommon strength and power or moral courage and fortitude. The word is widely used today to describe fictional characters with superpowers or those who have made sacrifices serving their country in the armed forces. Bolman and Deal highlight the danger of taking the hero metaphor too far in our understanding of leadership:

> A familiar archetypal image of the hero is the autonomous, lonely individual wandering on the fringes of society – the Lone Ranger, Dirty Harry or Rambo. This view taints our images of leadership. Would-be heroes pay a heavy personal price: alienation, feelings of failure, stress-induced illness, and early death. Organizations and institutions suffer and splutter because we ask too much of our leaders and too little of ourselves. (2001: 62)

Certain models or understandings of leadership can lead to a desire to be in some way 'heroic'. The 'would-be-heroes' described above can all too easily lose the sense of who they are called to be in the desire to make a name for themselves or fulfil the unrealistic expectations of others.

Pete, a 23-year-old youth minister, described the sense of exhaustion he felt in trying to maintain the image of a 'together and spiritually dynamic' leader. For him, the pressure came from the perceived expectations of other church leaders which resulted in him putting huge amounts of pressure on himself. Struggling to find safe places to explore some of the doubts he was experiencing, he ended up applying for jobs outside the Church and is now working in a school context.

Being a role model

One aspect of archetypal heroes is that the reader of the story can identify with them in some way. Often in modern literature heroes are ordinary people who end up facing extraordinary circumstances. We see in the popularity of children's books, such as J. K. Rowling's *Harry Potter* novels, the way in which children connect with particular characters – drawing parallels to their own lives and experiences. This kind of 'grounded' heroism is perhaps more akin to what we are talking about. Being a role model for young people is part of the job, whether we like it or not. Yasmin, who has been involved in youth ministry for ten years, has seen several of her young people pursue careers in youth ministry. She has been both encouraged and humbled as they have spoken of being inspired by her example.

Research suggests that role models who are followed as leaders tend to have the following characteristics:

- They have strength.
- They are in some way 'like' those following them.
- They have personal warmth.
- They are imperfect 'coping models' as opposed to being perfect (Cloud 2006: 92).

In today's culture much emphasis is placed on the external – how people look, their achievements, money, possessions, qualifications or how famous they are. If we are not careful we can buy into these values when it comes to understanding Christian leadership. Leadership qualities – even those which are positive and godly – can become attributes that we 'put on' like pieces of clothing, and our focus can be leadership 'trappings' such as being well known or having power and influence and visibility. There is a danger in adopting a personality – or 'persona' – which is different from who we essentially are, because we somehow believe that's what leaders should be like.

Looking at biblical examples encourages us that leaders come in all shapes and sizes, from diverse backgrounds and experience and with different approaches. Some individuals embrace and relish the opportunity to lead, others appear to be dragged kicking and screaming by the Holy Spirit into a leadership role. Some appear to be naturally gifted, others struggle to develop the skills required. We are called, first and foremost, to be ourselves, to become the unique individuals God created us to be and to allow him to change and transform us by his Holy Spirit, so that we can reach our potential and fulfil his purposes.

One fundamental aspect of our role is that our leadership is grounded in relationships with young people. These relationships are different from many of our other relationships. Kerry Young (1999), exploring the nature of these intentional relationships, describes youth workers as being like a friend to young people, but with significant differences. Our relationships may feel like friendships (and indeed may later develop into friendships) but we are not the young people's friends in the same way their peers are – we don't socialize with them in the same way. We are present in the relationship for their sakes and we make ourselves available for them. Although we will inevitably learn and receive from them, the relationship exists for their benefit and not to meet our needs.

Values of Christian leadership

With this understanding as a foundation for our thinking, we can go on to explore some of the key aspects and attributes of leaders.

Serving

Ministry is primarily about serving, first serving God and then serving others. Jesus himself not only talks about the importance of serving (Matthew 20.25–28; Matthew 23.8–12), but also models it as he washes his disciples' feet (John 13.1–17). Some of our serving as leaders may be visible, but much of our serving is likely to take place in unseen situations. We are likely to be the first to arrive and the last to leave when there are activities and events going on and jobs that need to be done. A lot of the time these two aspects of leadership – the visible and invisible – will happen concurrently, but there may be times and seasons where the emphasis is on one or the other. The important thing is to know that we are being obedient to God in how and where we are serving.

Pointing to Jesus

Although leadership is ultimately about being followed, our primary aim is to encourage people to follow Jesus. I love the attitude of John the Baptist, who, when his disciples moaned that Jesus was getting more attention and gaining more followers, said, 'He must become greater; I must become less' (John 3.30, NIV). He was confident in the ministry he had been given, but fundamentally understood his role in relation to who Jesus was and what Jesus was doing.

Autonomy

'The fact is that showing people who you are requires a degree of self-knowledge (or at least self-awareness) *as well as* self-disclosure. One without the other is hopeless' (Goffee and Jones 2006: 31). In leadership roles there is a need for a sense of who we are, for self-awareness and confidence in God. We have already noted the importance of developing and growing in God, but it is important to emphasize the need to gain security and confidence in Christ and our calling to serve him. Insecurity is incredibly destructive in leadership contexts as it can lead to competitiveness, anxiety and abuse of power. Becoming secure means having a realistic sense of who we are – our strengths and weaknesses – and an understanding that our responsibilities are God-given. We need to ensure that our sense of identity does not come from the position we hold, the power we exercise or the work we do but rather from who we are in God.

Collaboration

Coupled with a sense of autonomy and an ability to be self-directed is the need to work effectively with others. Bolman and Deal highlight the importance of our relationships for those who have leadership responsibilities:

Leadership is a relationship rooted in community. Leaders embody their group's most precious values and beliefs. Their ability to lead emerges from the strength and sustenance of those around them. It persists and deepens as they learn to use life's wounds to discover their own spiritual centers. As they conquer the demons within, they achieve the inner peace and bedrock confidence that enable them to inspirit and inspire others.   (2001: 62–3)

As we seek to outwork youth work principles of empowerment, equality of opportunity and participation, it is essential that we increase our capacity to work collaboratively through accountability, team work, consultation, effective delegation, identifying gifts, training, developing and releasing others.

Stewardship

As those given responsibility by God, we are stewards of all he has entrusted to us. This means that we need to commit ourselves to working in ways that safeguard those for whom we have responsibility and that promote their well-being. Part of this is about creating and sustaining safe space. Practically, this involves being aware of and implementing appropriate safeguarding and health and safety policies and procedures, not begrudgingly and reluctantly but because they assist us in being effective and working professionally and ethically. They will also assist in ensuring that our work is respected by those who operate in professional contexts outside our churches and organizations.

Character

In business and in all of life, reality demands come across one's path. And just as the 'character' of the metal determines whether that airplane is going to succeed in that kind of heat or torque, a person's character determines whether he or she will succeed in that situation. Their makeup, their integrity, will either be able to deliver or not. They will meet the demand, and succeed, leaving a wake of goals being reached and people being fulfilled only if their character can meet that demand.   (Cloud 2006: 24)

The issue of character is fundamental to leadership. Many gifted and talented individuals have been incredibly successful in ministry and then found themselves floundering because of character issues. If we are to be role models to young people, who we are is going to speak much more loudly than what we do. Our integrity is what will really make a difference in the long term.

Developing and releasing others

A crucial value for those with any leadership role is that of developing and releasing others to fulfil their potential in God. As leaders we should be identifying, acknowledging and honouring the giftedness we see in those who work with us and in the young people we serve. It is important that we recognize a breadth of gifts, but in this context it is relevant to highlight the need to nurture leadership gifts. As role models, we are likely to find that young people want to follow in our footsteps, and providing both encouragement and safe spaces to explore and develop skills is crucial. This may involve meaningful, supportive delegation of tasks and responsibilities and/or the involvement of young people in leadership teams, decision-making and planning processes. We may strategically set about mentoring young people into leadership roles, working with them to encourage their growth and development. When I was working in church-based youth ministry my goal was to consistently do myself out of a job, and this necessitated not only identifying others who were gifted in leadership but also supporting them to develop these gifts, encouraging them when things went wrong or right, praying with and for them, training and nurturing where needed and being explicit about the processes of youth work – for example, those unseen things that form the foundation of the work, like prayer, preparation, relationship building and practical or administrative tasks.

Leadership styles and roles

As we have already noted, leadership is exercised in many different ways and our preferred styles and approaches will be influenced by our upbringing, values, personality, culture, church background, motivations and what we have seen modelled ourselves. Other chapters in this book explore some of these issues in more depth, but it is helpful to highlight some key models and styles here.

Up-front, visionary leadership

Some leaders receive a clear vision from God and then take a strong lead in taking people forward to fulfil that vision. Moses, Joshua, Deborah and David would all exemplify this style, as leaders who have a clear sense of what God is saying and devote themselves to leading the people to fulfil the vision.

Managerial leadership

This approach uses organizational skills to identify a need, develop strategy, recruit support and undertake the work, delegating responsibility and using evaluation processes to assess the ongoing effectiveness. One biblical example for this style would be Nehemiah, who demonstrates an ability to think and act strategically to rebuild Jerusalem's walls.

Overseeing leadership

An important aspect of leadership, which may form a key role for some, is that of overseeing. This involves having a broader perspective of the work and the context than those around us and being able to hold in tension the different needs, expectations, values and pressures that come from this. A biblical example is found in the way that Paul writes to the young churches in the New Testament.

Intercessory leadership

We may be called to an intercessory or advocacy-type leadership role, like Esther, who finds herself in a position of influence 'at such a time as this' (Esther 4.14) and uses that influence on behalf of God's people.

Facilitative leadership

We may be called to lead in a way that facilitates, encourages and empowers the ministry of others. We see evidence of this in the way Jesus trains, releases and sends out his disciples (Luke 10).

Use of power

Some of these styles of leadership find easy parallels in leadership theory as we observe the spectrum of approaches in terms of use of power. Although power can often be perceived as a negative thing, it is an inevitable aspect of having a leadership role. Whether we want it or not, whether we feel powerful or not, the position we hold will automatically give us power in relation to others. How we use this power is what makes it either positive or negative. It is helpful here to consider different approaches to the use of power in leadership roles:

- authoritarian – the leader has power, makes all the decisions, the people follow;
- authoritative – the leader takes a strong lead and makes clear decisions but engages with others in the process;
- consultative – the leader makes clear decisions but consults with others through the process and the decisions are informed by this consultation;
- collaborative – decisions are made through discussion, negotiation and agreement;
- democratic – decisions are made democratically with the majority having the final say;
- laissez faire – from the French 'leave to do', this laid-back style sometimes comes with over-delegating;
- chaotic – the leader abdicates all responsibility and lets people get on with it.

In a youth work context it would be difficult to see any value in either of the extreme styles of leadership. An authoritarian approach would appear to mitigate against empowerment and any genuine participation and a chaotic style could lead to unsafe practice. However, although we may have our own preferred style, we may find ourselves needing to use any of the others as we encounter different situations. For example, my preference may be a collaborative approach, but if there is a fire in the building I am going to be authoritative and ensure that everyone gets out quickly!

Authenticity

We will need to grow in skill and expertise if we are to be effective leaders – training, reflection, support from others, feedback and self-awareness will all help this process. In considering who we are as leaders I am convinced that the breadth of models, styles and examples gives us freedom to develop approaches that fit who we are as individuals. It is crucial that we don't simply try to be a carbon copy of someone we admire, weary ourselves with endless comparisons or endlessly try to fit a model that doesn't suit us. We need to find ways of leading which reflect and express our skills, personality and character.

In a church he worked for, Steve found himself under incredible pressure to be an extrovert, up-front type of leader. He related well to the young people, developed effective mentoring relationships and established good networks and relationships in the local community. However, the criticism he experienced led to him becoming discouraged, and when his contract came to an end he found a job with another church in which his style and personality were valued and appreciated.

In a similar vein, although we will inevitably be a role model for young people, our intention in working with them shouldn't be to produce clones of ourselves who think and behave like us, but to assist them in becoming the unique individuals God has created them to be. They will be different from us, with their own unique personalities, ideas, beliefs, values and dreams, and this is important. We should be encouraging people to conform to the image of Christ and not to our image.

Having said that, we should be examples for young people of what it means to grow, learn and be disciples of Christ. Being a 'flawed hero' means sharing our imperfections and our struggles with young people, as well as our successes. It is about forgoing the temptation to present a facade of a 'perfect' Christian, who never has any problems, has an amazing spiritual life and is full of faith and power. The reality is that at times we all struggle. This calls for wisdom. We need to strike a healthy balance between appropriate self-disclosure, helpful self-revelation and maintaining healthy personal and professional boundaries. This means that we should not pour out our vulnerabilities on to the young people, or burden them with our needs – but that the person they meet should be authentic, not a false image or projection.

So without seeking comfort and burdening them, we can be open about times we have struggled; without manipulating them, we can share our frailties; without unnerving or embarrassing them, we can be open about our temptations. Our relationships with young people are not the place where we get our needs met – we sort out appropriate support for that – but they can be instrumental in modelling what it means to live as a Christian in the pressures, uncertainties and complexity of today's world.

Henry Cloud, in exploring issues of integrity, talks about a 'dynamic tension between power and vulnerability' (2006: 88). For us as leaders, embracing with humility the power that God has given us and choosing with confidence to work in vulnerability will assist us in following the example of Christ, who was the perfect example of godly, servant leadership.

Questions for reflection

- When you think about leadership, which character (or characters) from the Bible do you find you relate to? Why?
- What values are important to you as a leader? How are these expressed in the way you lead?
- How would you describe your own leadership style? How has this developed?
- How do you feel about being a role model for young people? What issues, questions, encouragements or pressures does this raise for you?

References and further reading

Bolman, L. G. and Deal, T. E., 2001. *Leading with Soul: An uncommon journey of spirit*. San Francisco, Jossey Bass.

Cloud, H., 2006. *Integrity: The courage to meet the demands of reality*. New York, HarperCollins. Excellent book to read to help understand the importance of integrity in the whole of our lives.

Dean, K. C. and Foster, R., 1998. *The Godbearing Life: The art of soul tending for youth ministry*. Nashville, Upper Rooms Books. Helpful reflections on the spiritual life of leaders in youth ministry.

Goffee, R. and Jones, G., 2006. *Why Should Anyone Be Led by You? What it takes to be an authentic leader*. Boston, Harvard Business School.

Hassall, R., 2009. *Growing Young Leaders*. Abingdon, Bible Reading Fellowship. Helps us to nurture leadership in the young people we work with.

Nouwen, H. J. M., 1994. *The Wounded Healer*. London, Darton, Longman and Todd. Spiritual classic full of inspired wisdom and deep truths about how we can minister out of who we are.

Watson, A., 1999. *The Fourfold Leadership of Jesus: Come, follow, wait, go*. Abingdon, Bible Reading Fellowship. Biblically rooted exploration of four ways of being a Christian leader.

Young, K., 1999. *The Art of Youth Work*. Lyme Regis, Russell House.

3

Visionary architect

> Architecture is the masterly, correct, and magnificent play of forms
> under the light.   (Le Corbusier)

Those of us who have watched Channel 4's *Grand Designs* will have
joined Kevin McLeod's journeys with the adventurous and the
obsessed towards the (re)construction of their dream homes. Serious
time and attention is spent in the designing, planning phase of the
building process – in fact, often longer than the actual construction.
Not only are the function and the aesthetic qualities carefully considered, but also the lifespan of what is built. How will the building
respond to changes in the inhabitants' lives? What materials will be
used in the building and how are they to be sourced? How energy-
efficient is the building, and is this sustainable? Even aesthetics has
a strange kind of moral quality – is it 'right' to build a certain kind
of building in a particular location? A range of practical and ethical
considerations need to be made.

There are many resonances here in relation to building and shaping a youth ministry. My view is that, particularly if youth workers
are developing new projects or renewing old ones, not taking time
to seriously consider the relevance of the kinds of questions that have

been hinted at above in relation to what is 'made' with young people, and what will be required to make it, would seem foolish. When the crowds gathered around Christ (Luke 14.28–30), his basic point of wisdom was just that: before building, *consider the cost* – gain clarity about what it is you are getting into and what it's going to mean for all involved. We would be mistaken if this was taken as a point of encouragement, as these words are preceded by a painful statement about what it *would* cost, designed to shock, and to make those first hearers stop and reflect, and reconsider. On a practical level, investing ourselves in architectural processes enables us ultimately to build sustainable, inspiring and sound ministries that the local church owns.

What I am aiming to do in this chapter is to intersperse my reflections on being a visionary architect with a case study following a process of developing a church- and community-based youth ministry. This case study is for illustrative purposes, as there are, and will continue to be, a multitude of creative contextual responses to developing work with young people. I have structured the chapter around a particular kind of planning process, which, again, is one way of approaching this. For me, processes like these, entered into openly and prayerfully, are extremely helpful in discerning what is 'right' within a particular context.

In him we live and move and design the building

I want to return at this point to the quote that opened this chapter, and pursue this idea of the 'light' under (or within) which a youth ministry is built. The shape and structure of any building has the ability to convey a certain kind of quality of light within it. This is self-evident simply through observation. The decisions made by the architect are crucial in determining this. Without wanting to push the metaphor too far, there is the potential to plan and build something that allows no light inside. Equally, there is the potential to build a structure that, because of its relationship to the light, allows the qualities of light to be appreciated in ways never before experienced. Such is the responsibility of the architect; he or she is in a position to have an impact on people's living experience of light. It is often said that young people draw conclusions about the Christian faith based on the kinds of experiences they have when they encounter it. The 'light' in this case is that of the personhood of the Trinitarian God at the heart of the Christian faith. Ministry therefore begins, is energized by and finds its fulfilment in the self-giving love of God and his desire and capacity to redeem all things. This is the light we sculpt and design within. Seeing our local mission (our purpose in the present) as inspired by a biblical hope for the renewal of the whole of creation (2 Peter 3.13) is the beginning of our envisioning. This reality can also liberate us from attachment to particular structures, approaches or methods, and enable us when appropriate to redesign the building, both in response to the 'light' and also in response to social and cultural change. For those seeking to develop a youth ministry, this will involve doing some theological thinking, and creative playfulness in addition to some prayerful seeking.

The strategic planning process

Strategic plans are not wish-lists. They build on where you are now, and aim to develop a ministry in a particular direction. They need to pay attention to a range of contexts and available resources. Proper strategic planning is a staged process which takes legwork and effort, and requires commitment to a process of information-gathering, discernment and decision-making.

Stage one: selecting a team

Before proceeding much further, it is wise to draw together the right team of people to lead this process. This is for a number of reasons:

- *Delegation* – the sharing of the workload – may take anywhere up to three months, and involve a significant quantity of time and legwork.
- *Appropriate participation or representation* – involving people who already have informal or formal contact with those to be consulted at the next stage in this process – also affords the opportunity to involve one or two young people at an early stage, and ensures (proving the right environment is set) that they can represent the perspective of their peers.
- *Shared skills* – combining skill sets, and working in pairs or individually on tasks in between team meetings ensures that those most

able to complete a task are allowed to do so. This is reflective of the apostle Paul's teaching to the church in Corinth; we need other people to effectively be church (1 Corinthians 12).

- *Shared insight* – this highlights the issue that this process is ultimately one of discernment, choosing those people who will work together to listen to the context and to the varied voices, to bring their existing understanding to bear on the process, and to be open to the leading of the Spirit. These principles are evident in the life of the early Church in Acts 6.1–7, in the churches' collaborative identification of those most suited to take on management responsibility for the just distribution of food.

Case study: Stage one
A team was put together comprising

- the current part-time student youth worker;
- two young people, male and female;
- the curate;
- a parent of young people who was also a member of the PCC and had a background in a profession within the social sector;
- two experienced youth workers, both of whom had lived in the community for at least five years and had worked in a variety of contexts. One of these acted as team leader.

Stage two: understanding the environment
Given that it is impossible to know and analyse everything, the aim at this stage is to gain enough of an understanding to be able to develop the work with respect to *what is actually going on in the real world*. In terms of our architectural metaphor, this is essentially gathering knowledge and understanding in order to avoid planning an inaccessible or inappropriate structure.

The broader social and political context
Essentially, this is about raising awareness of the larger currents in society that describe the overall social context of work with young people. One of the familiar tools to break this down into more distinct

areas is known as a PEST analysis (see <www.quickmba.com/strategy/pest/>). This acronym denotes the following headings, and included in the list are two examples of the kinds of questions that may be worth pursuing in each area:

1 Political:
   (a) What are the current government policy frameworks that are specifically targeted at young people generally?
   (b) What are the current legal contexts for work with young people?
2 Economic:
   (a) What are the current employment prospects of young people following school or higher education?
   (b) What funding is available, from either statutory bodies or charitable trusts, for work with young people?
3 Socio-cultural:
   (a) What recent historical events have had an impact on the views, perspectives and attitudes of young people towards other groups in society, and vice versa?
   (b) What are prevailing attitudes among young people towards religion and spirituality?
4 Technological:
   (a) What is the role of technology in shaping young people's social interaction?
   (b) How has the democratization of information on the internet affected the role of the 'old' authoritative institutions such as the Church?

The local geographic community

Community profiling (Hawtin and Smith 2007) is an activity used by a range of different organizations in order to gain an understanding of the nature of a specific community and what it is like to live in it. It is used by local governments for a variety of purposes, usually relating to the redistribution of resources or shaping local services. It is also used by voluntary or community organizations as a means of mapping change and holding local government accountable for interventions, but also to develop a case to support funding bids. The understanding that profiling brings is crucial in terms of the kind of strategic planning that is under discussion here. For these reasons, a little research may result in an existing published profile being found in a local library.

Community profiles are likely to contain hard (statistical) data about lifestyle, wealth, levels of deprivation, employment, demographics and ethnicity, among other things. They also will contain soft (subjective) data – opinions, thoughts and feelings that residents have regarding the community they live in. In addition, information may exist regarding existing provision for young people in the locality.

The local church

On the assumption that the local Christian communities will be the main funder, possible employer of staff and main source of volunteer assistance, a good understanding of them needs to be developed. Some churches will have an established and accepted mission or vision statement, which will be a critical reference point for the youth ministry they resource. It is often the case that parents of young people who are part of the Christian community are those who push forward a youth work agenda within the church. As a major stakeholder, their expectations also need to be understood, particularly in relation to how they hope their own children will benefit from any youth specific provision.

Young people

If there are young people already engaged in the project, then hopefully those working with them will have a reasonably well-developed sense of their backgrounds, aspirations and interests and role in the local and/or faith community. If this is not the case, then it may require some detached work, or research through a local school, to develop understanding of this area. The ability to empathize with young people is necessarily proceeded by developing an understanding of what may be going on in their lives. For example, is the stereotypical 'storm and stress' model of adolescence an accurate reflection of young people's experiences and behaviour? Do we relate to young people as if they are 'deficient', or as if they are 'developing'? The answers to these questions will help us to recognize what underpinning assumptions are present in the ways in which adults will seek to develop relationships with young people.

Case study: Stage two

- The team were able to pool their existing knowledge and under-standing of young people and current national contexts for youth work.
- A community audit had been published two years previously, giving a fairly up-to-date account of the geographic community.
- The student youth worker had already produced a brief profile for a university assignment, focusing on the experience of young people living in the local community and the provision available.
- The parent and the curate were able to share their understanding of the vision and mission of the Christian community.

Stage three: consultation with stakeholders

Consultation aims to gain an insight into how various stakeholders may want to see a particular project develop, understanding both their priorities and the way they may want to relate to the work once it starts. These groups of people are likely to be key people in terms of resourcing and developing the work, or the main beneficiaries of it. There are a number of ways of carrying out consultation, as there are with any kind of research, but the important question is how to make sure that

1 those consulted speak to you honestly about hopes, fears and expectations;
2 what they do say has a meaningful role in ultimately shaping what is done.

The worst kind of consultation appears as *tokenism*. This is where stakeholders are involved only to check whether a predetermined path would be resisted or simply to make them *feel* valued when in reality what they say is disregarded. For example, frequently youth ministry is seen as something *done to* rather than *done with* or *done for* young people. Likewise, if the work is going to embody a theology of servanthood, then it is at this point in the process that this com-mitment will start to be evident in the actions of those leading the planning process – they will seek to serve those most impacted, in ways which are relevant to their roles. One of the dangers at this point is that frequently people identify those things that they *already know and are comfortable with* as being appropriate for the future. Part of this process eventually may be to communicate a coherent rationale as to why you are *not* going to carry out the wishes and desires of the stakeholders in the shape and direction of the ministry.

Case study: Stage three

- Questionnaires were circulated to all members of the church, to ascertain what they believed to be priorities.
- Personal contact and face-to-face meetings were made with the statutory youth centre and local schools.
- A questionnaire was designed by young people on the team to take to young people already connected to the youth ministry.
- Conversations were held with the existing small team of volunteers and the existing part-time youth worker.
- Personal contact was made with the Parish Council and local police.
- Church leaders (the vicar and the curate) were invited to comment from their perspective.

Stage four: defining the qualities and structure of the building

At this stage, identifying and piecing together the basic aspects of the structure of the building can begin. This involves clearly identifying focal areas of the work and the essential priorities in each area. The issue of approach in youth ministry is rightly contested territory, because many approaches are valid and have coherent and established arguments to substantiate them. Mark Senter (2001) identifies six questions; in the list below, I see the first three as forming the basis for reflection in this area, while the fourth is my own.

1 In what ways might the youth ministry connect with the church? (E.g. through the activity of volunteer youth workers? Through using the same building? Through shared beliefs? Through meaningful contact with others in the community?)

2 What roles do adults play in this process? (E.g. authority figures or permission-givers? Models of godly life? Spiritual mentors? Teachers? Entertainers?)

3 What roles do young people play? (E.g. submissive followers? Prophetic voices? Students? Partners in ministry and mission?)
4 If appropriate, what role might an employed full-time youth worker play? (Read this book for some stimulating ideas!)

A number of practitioners in the field of youth ministry have conceptualized responses to these kinds of questions. It is likely to be appropriate to blend a number of these approaches according to the outcomes of the previous stages of the strategic planning process. The choices at this point will shape the basic theology and philosophy of the work. It may be helpful to think of these as 'maps', so that Christian youth work is seen as:

- work facilitating an intergenerational faith community (Nel 2001; Gardner 2008);
- a fluid interpersonal spiritual practice (Yaconelli 2007);
- a preparation for service and ministry in the faith community (Black 1998);
- work that leads to the strategic developing of youth congregations (Senter 2001);
- work that engages the passions and longings of young people in their seeking of God in community (Dean 2004);
- a missional practice which takes place beyond the existing structures of church (Ward 1997; Passmore 2003);
- work that engages in a process of community development with, or on behalf of, young people (Bowyer 2004);
- formal, semi-formal or informal schools' work (Jackson 2003);
- outdoor education (Smith 1994).

___

Case study: Stage four
A blend of the following approaches was articulated, in order of emphasis:

- fluid interpersonal spiritual practice
- facilitating an intergenerational faith community
- preparation for service and ministry in the faith community
- semi-formal schools' work
- community development (providing a service).

___

Stage five: fixtures and fittings

Finally, it is necessary to select the events that facilitate the kinds of interactions that are hoped for, between young people themselves, volunteers or workers and young people, and finally young people and the wider community or world. A broad and integrated set of events need to be combined to produce a holistic educational experience for young people. In addition, there will be some of the following, which clearly are a better fit for choices in the previous stage. Decisions made at this point need to take into account the available resources, and the skill base of volunteers and staff. Further training may be needed to equip people to support particular activities, which may include:

- small group work
- an open youth club
- mentoring or discipleship on a one-to-one basis
- detached youth work
- peer education
- information provision
- sports activities
- a youth forum
- life skills workshops
- gender-specific work
- community action projects
- developing music and arts facilities
- campaigning and/or fundraising
- exercising gifts within the faith community alongside adults.

Case study: Stage five

A blend of the following events was chosen in order to effectively fulfil the strategy:

- peer/adult-led small group structures
- mentoring/discipleship on a one-to-one basis
- gender-specific work
- community action projects
- exercising gifts within the faith community alongside adults
- detached youth work
- life skills workshops in secondary schools
- an open youth club.

They varied in terms of frequency and emphasis in order to reflect the priorities.

Conclusion

This may seem like a protracted process, but the foundations are the most important part of the building. It is something that needs to be fully revisited every three to five years in order to ensure that what is being invested in is still well aligned with contexts, stakeholders and the values embedded in approach. The internal and external goods (the thinking and the paperwork) that this produces will be a valuable resource for a range of other activities of the project, such as defining job descriptions, applying for funding or discerning whether or not to partner with another organization. Whether you are thinking about a small church-based youth work or a large organization-based project, time invested in planning and strategy is vital – a visionary architect is needed to help your work fulfil its potential.

Questions for reflection

- What do you think it would mean for you and your team to revisit questions of vision and strategy?
- How might you better understand the needs and aspirations of young people in your community?
- On a scale of 1 to 10, how well do you think your church knows and understands what you do now and what your hopes for the future are? How might you increase this shared sense of vision?
- What structures and activities need to be redesigned in your current practice?

References and further reading

Black, W., 1998. *An Introduction to Youth Ministry*. Nashville, Broadman and Holman.

Bowyer, P., 2004. *Express Community*. Carlisle, Authentic.

Dean, K. C., 2004. *Practicing Passion*. Grand Rapids, Eerdmans.

Gardner, J., 2008. *Mend the Gap: Can the Church reconnect the generations?* Nottingham, IVP.

Hawtin, M. and Percie Smith, J., 2007. *Community Profiling: Auditing social needs*. Buckingham, Open University Press. Helpful if you need to start from scratch in assessing community needs.

Jackson, L., 2003. *Effective Schools Work*. Eastbourne, Kingsway.

Nel, M., 2001. 'Youth ministry: an inclusive congregational approach', in M. Senter (ed.) *Four Views of Youth Ministry and the Church*. Grand Rapids, Zondervan.

Passmore, R., 2003. *Meet Them Where They're At*. Bletchley, Scripture Union.

Pimlott, N., 2007. *How to Develop a Youth Work Project: Lessons from Noah*. Cambridge, Grove. Accessible overview to planning a new project.

Senter, M. (ed.), 2001. *Four Views of Youth Ministry and the Church*. Grand Rapids, Zondervan.

Smith, A., 1994. *Creative Outdoor Work with Young People*. Lyme Regis, Russell House Publishing.

Ward, P., 1997. *Youthwork and the Mission of God*. London, SPCK. Explores two of the main ways that we do youth work.

Yaconelli, M., 2007. *Growing Souls: Experiments in contemplative youth ministry*. London, SPCK.

4

Community builder

NICK SHEPHERD

> Community is not a question of choice. To be human is to live
> in community, in relationship. Divine intimacy is the final goal of
> one's total being ... The questions for us are: How well will I live in
> community? How visible in my life is the example of Christ? Can
> we be the visible sign of God's action in the world today through
> our own witness to community? (Sofield *et al.*)

Youth work or youth ministry should always be undertaken in
response to young people. Whatever agendas youth workers hold,
and there are always some, the situations, struggles and suggestions
of young people should create the context for youth work. For youth
work to be Christian we need to look through theological eyes into
the 'physical, emotional, academic, social, economic and spiritual
needs of young people' (Borgman 1997: 228) and act on our insights
as missionary, educator and pastor. In this chapter I will argue that
the roles of missionary, educator and pastor are ones that can only
be properly fulfilled within community. 'Community' is a rich term
with many possible implications for Christian youth work. I use it
here to mean a group of young people and adults who are connected
in an ongoing, shared life which is directed towards a common purpose:

what some would call a 'community of practice'. An excellent exploration of this concept is seen in Lave and Wenger (1991) and their work underpins some of the thinking in this chapter.

Forming and participating in community is an end in and of itself within mission. Community building is not a tool for youth work, but a goal. How we engage in community building will depend on the context we are trying to impact or serve. Community is at the heart of mission because community is central to the very nature of God as Trinity. The community of persons in the Trinity (Father, Son and Holy Spirit) is the template for action and attitudes in the Church. If the Church is to glorify God (which is its purpose) then being a community 'who love one another' is our purpose (Grenz 1994: 632–64). It is this life of love that is extended to others in mission. In fact, the word 'mission' was first used to describe the way in which the persons of the Trinity are mutually serving and sustaining (Bosch 1991: 11). Now we use it to mean being sent by God into the world to serve and sustain others. There is no separation here between a loving church community acting in the world and the kingdom of God advancing – they are one and the same (Grenz 1994: 655). When we invite others to participate in this community we are inviting them to participate in the life of love of God. As varied communities in different contexts, 'churches' also have a shared life that celebrates, questions and enacts this love. Inviting people to participate in this life is 'life-changing': a provocation or a confrontation. Being in the community of Christ should be naturally evangelistic. Mission and community go together. What we mean by 'community', though, can be trickier to define.

Christian communities of practice – sensing, shaping and sustaining faith

Building community can mean many different things. In terms of youth work it can refer to the way in which youth leaders can act to enable young people to participate in church as an intergenerational community (Green and Green 2000; Gardner 2008). It can refer to the task of supporting young people to understand more about the needs of their local community, and empowering them to express their hopes and frustrations as well as to act to be the solutions to some of these needs (Packham 2008). These are both excellent goals and ones that deserve attention. In this chapter, though, I am focusing on a particular task: how Christian youth work functions to provide young people with a community within which they can engage in the task of 'trying to be Christian'.

'Being community' in this sense is sometimes given a narrower definition of that of 'a community of practice'. Communities of practice are specific gatherings of people where the focus of the community is to pass on or sustain a way of life, or support specific skills and functions in a wider social world. How people learn to become expert builders or butchers, how arts groups become the focus for a person's sense of identity and belonging and how the Church sustains the memory of the gospel and seeks to make this known to others, can all be understood through these being examples of communities of practice. Within such places people can find a sense of belonging, practical support for pressures they face, good fun, challenging people, stimulating conversation, meaningful activities such as art, prayer and computer games and, above all, a space where they can engage in a vital personal task – working out who they are and want to be.

Simply extending this understanding to how we might participate in church as a way of learning and growing in faith is perhaps obvious. However, to talk of youth groups specifically as being communities of practice requires developing how we might understand the Church as operating as a community of practice, or rather communities of practice, and how it is through building appropriate groups for young people to participate that Christian youth work acts to stimulate, shape and sustain a faith of young people to a faith of their own.

Places to stimulate faith

The understanding of the Church as the community of God's people has caused theologians over the ages to fall out. It continues to be a divisive debate: questions arise over who is in and who is out, whether we should adopt fresh expressions or faithful practices, and if activities such as youth work serve to form or fracture the Church. One reason why such arguments persist is actually because our understanding of the Church, and our experience of being church, keeps changing. James Fowler, whom we know best from faith development theory, suggests that this is because a central task to the Church is actually to keep changing. Not that the Church should move away from the central calling to be God's people and to seek to understand and express the gospel as best we can, but that the Church should be constantly adapting to maintain its presence in the world. By this he means that the Church is always innovating in how it meets, understands worship, engages in mission and undertakes teaching (Fowler 1999). Such innovation can be identified in concrete terms through time – the development of medieval religious orders; the use of music hall songs in Victorian mission; the popularity of the Alpha Course. Youth work too can be viewed as an innovation to maintain and extend Christian presence among young people. Through Christian youth work the Church acts to make herself known, and thus to extend Christian presence, into the world of young people. This is true from the perspective of youth work inside and outside the Church. Within the Church, youth work creates a space where young people who have been nurtured in faith can act themselves to own faith. In extending work to those beyond the Church, Christian youth work can engage in mission with young people with little or no understanding of faith to invite them to experience and explore the story and community of faith – the essence of being church.

Places to support faith

The role of community in the formation of religious identity has long been seen as important. John Westerhoff (2009) explores how children and young people form a personal faith through participation in purposeful communities of faith. For Westerhoff, people sense faith for themselves best when they encounter faith in others. Yet, as Western society has evolved, this formation has moved from a passive adoption of values and beliefs to one which requires a more active engagement. This is in part because broader structures in society (school, media, state) do not provide strong affirmation of religious identity. Sociologist Duncan MacLaren (2004) suggests that this requires people to make a specific choice to hold to a faith identity, whether they have been raised as believers or not. He also stresses that this choice is one that is faced in particular by the young. He goes on to suggest that in mission and discipleship the Church thus faces a task of building 'plausibility shelters' – social structures (groups, networks, events, media) to reinforce the possibility of holding a faith identity. In short, belonging is becoming more and more an element of believing, not a precursor. This means that the structures we build in youth work are important – whether these are cell groups for young Christians or 'drop-in centres' for outreach. Youth work can quite literally create places to be Christian.

Places to shape faith

Youth work has long held to the view that the social context in which people are taught shapes the way in which this education affects them (Young 2006). The way in which education functions within the Church has in recent times become more sensitive to understanding the importance of participation in church as community, not simply in the importance of acts such as preaching or Sunday School teaching. Elaine Graham provides a description of how participation in a community of faith influences beliefs, values and identity. Graham argues that individuals act within specific groups to develop their understanding of self in relation to God. Such groups she calls Intentional Christian Community. This is preferable to a term such as 'church' or 'congregation' because it describes a functioning aspect of Christian community – an identifiable gathering through which a group of Christians are trying to make sense of faith and share together in activities that make God known (1996: 147). For Graham it is not just that these groups exist which is important, but that they are engaged in practices that seek to make sense of their experience of faith and seek to encounter God in meaningful ways to their situation of life.

The practices that Graham talks about include preaching, but importantly also revolve around formal and informal sharing of the personal experience of faith. By drawing on Christian practices such as prayer, worship and biblical insight, people don't just learn about God but come to know faith. Participation in the practices of faith communities 'gives rise to new knowledge' (1996: 99), serves to reinforce self-identity (1996: 166) and makes God known.

The notion of communities of practice provides a helpful way of viewing the task and purpose of being 'church'. A crucial question for Christian youth work, then, is how this communal life can be built so that young people can see, stimulate, support and sustain a life of faith. To explore this I will draw next on the experience of two quite different young people.

Creating places to be Christian:
youth groups as communities of practice

Youth work as building a community of practice where young people can participate in owning and expressing a faith of their own is seen in the following accounts from two young people – Gerard and Bryony. These two young people start their faith journey from quite different places, but for both of them it is belonging and acting in community that is significant in moving them on.

Gerard

Gerard is 17. He's been a Christian all his life – in fact he talks about being Christian as something that is 'ingrained' in his sense of self. His family are committed and involved in church, his best friends are the young people he has grown up with in the church and he has never really had any points of crisis that have shaken his faith. Despite this, being a Christian is something that Gerard struggles with. He struggles to know whether this is his faith or that of his parents; he struggles to know how to talk about this important and precious aspect of his life with school friends; and he feels under pressure all the time to 'be Christian' – to show this aspect of who he is without offending people, but with credibility. Without his youth group Gerard says he wouldn't be able to 'hack' being a Christian – he reckons he would have jacked it in. His group is the place he goes to 'be himself' – not to escape the problems he faces elsewhere, but to discuss them with friends, to pose questions to his leaders and to relate his hopes and fears to God through interactive prayer. Gerard's advice to any young Christian is that if you want to survive as a Christian you need to find a group like this.

Bryony

Bryony is also 17. She doesn't even describe herself as a Christian – yet. She says she wants to, but she doesn't feel that she knows enough about God. You might think she should: she's been on two Youth Alpha courses and is about to start her third, she can explain the Trinity and she has seen a number of her friends baptized. Bryony's even had some profound experiences of God. She used to engage in self-harming practices, cutting herself and drinking, but has found the capacity to stop this through prayer. She prays regularly and the launch pad for this transformation was going to a dedication service for one of her leader's children – it was such a special occasion, she feels, to see this loving family and community and to see the types of promises they were making for their son. The community that Bryony is beginning to feel a part of is formed around a drop-in project. It's a bunch of youth workers, young and older volunteers from local churches and a crowd of young people who live close by. Before coming here Bryony thought all Christians were weird – some still are, but not this lot. They're 'safe'. Safe because she can be herself here – talk about all that's wrong in her life. Safe because they're not odd, not religious, but do show her that if God can 'create such wonderful people' maybe he can change her as well.

What Gerard and Bryony illustrate is that being a Christian in today's world is a tough act. It's tough because the society we live in is inhospitable to faith: choosing to believe and growing in one's own understanding of self rooted as a person of faith requires a young person to wrestle with critical questions of identity. For Christian young people this is an activity that requires particular work – they have to work out what being a Christian means, not only in what beliefs about God they might hold but in what they believe about themselves. We can label this activity 'faith identity work' (Shepherd 2010). Gerard illustrates that some Christian young people respond to this pressure by finding and joining their own intentional Christian community within which they can undertake the complex task of working out what faith means to them, and also acting to support one another in expressing this faith.

Christian youth work, though, can also provide a space where young people who have had no previous connection to church can find faith for themselves. All young people, though to differing degrees, engage in some form of struggle over their understanding of self (Young 2006). Bryony shows that when a young person encounters a Christian community in which he or she can participate, it provides the opportunity for identity work that might lead to faith, as each individual engages with the identity-giving stories and practices within this community of practice. Savage *et al.* suggest that such a purpose – to be places where young people can encounter different narratives against (or within) which they can understand themselves – should be at the heart of Christian youth work (2006: 156–8).

Constructing a sense of place pays attention to what signals are being sent to young people about the values, aims and practices of the community they are being encouraged to encounter or form. Sense of place is created through the people who are there, the activities they engage in and the ways in which people are encouraged to participate. Maintaining a strong voluntary participation ethos is not in tension with this approach – in fact, it is essential. Once a community is formed that provides young people with a recognizable community that might meet the need or interest they have in engaging with faith, it is only through their active joining that this can be properly pursued. Joining, then, is the companion to building and is a way in which young people can exercise their choice to deepen or develop their own sense of faith identity.

Christian youth work that fosters a community within which young people can actively participate, and through which they can engage in their own activity to better understand themselves, is perhaps an obvious approach to take. The important point to grasp is that young people require specific types of youth work, with a particular group. This is the task of community building that lies before youth ministry – the task of building the most appropriate groups within which young people can form and express a sense of self as Christian.

The youth worker as community builder

To conclude this discussion of the importance of community building I want to focus on three skills, or rather practices, that foster such an approach. The first is *hospitality*, the second is *honesty* and the third is *humility* (see Table 4.1).

The first task of youth work as community building is being hospitable. Hospitality is a Christian practice with rich history and meaning (Pohl 1999). Centrally, here, it is about making space for young people. In order to create spaces that stimulate faith for young people we must first provide spaces that are hospitable to young people. This is something that churches are actually very good at. Opening up a church hall, raising money to create a drop-in centre, setting aside an evening in one's week to host games and run a tuck shop – these are all practical but influential acts that, when done

Table 4.1 Practices that foster community building

Hospitality	Honesty	Humility
• Asking young people how the Church can serve them	• Telling young people why we are interested in working with them	• Working in a team, as we can't do everything
• Adapting church life to be inclusive of young people	• Talking about ourselves and our faith	• Welcoming what young people bring to the life of a group
• Advocating for young people's needs and interests	• Taking seriously their experience of life and offering a place and space for reflection	• Watching how young people 'use' what we offer and adapting what we do
• Acting to provide space and time for young people to hang out together	• Trying ways of exploring spirituality and Christian belief that provoke questions	• Waiting to see if young people set new agendas for discussion and dialogue

within or from the community of faith, establish Christian presence in the world of young people and seek the life of God to spring from young people's lives (Dean and Foster 1998). Being hospitable means accepting young people for who they are, and how they are. This does not mean that no attempts are made to confront behaviours that damage or harm others, but crucially that the grounds for meeting are to welcome these young people as they are. This too can perhaps be an overlooked characteristic of church-based youth work. Too often assumptions and expectations of what Christian young people should be like become ideal rather than real. Being hospitable to church young people means making a space for doubt and frustration, for failure and restoration.

Whatever the style of work adopted, youth workers will usually 'provide' young people with sets of activities to be the basis for educational, recreational or personal development use. Yet talking remains at the heart of all such activity. Youth work that fosters intentional Christian community does so by provoking a conversation on what it means, or might mean, to be Christian. It is honest in being open to talk about why we are there, what hopes we have that participation might mean and what we think authentic faith looks and feels like. Here the Christian youth worker is involved in designing activities that might provoke engagement and reflection on self-esteem, be these specific acts of prayer or worship, teaching on biblical passages or theological concepts, or discussion on tricky questions or misconceptions. In each of these the skill of the community builder is to direct and not control the way in which such practices are engaged with, but to allow participation in these to shape conversation. Developing a conversation on what it means to be Christian gives space and support to young people who are exploring or choosing to act out their own faith (Bass and Richter 2002). Such 'God talk' can provoke young people to think through their lives and draw on the images and stories of faith to make sense of things (Nash *et al.* 2007). Beyond this, when young people start discussing the way in which God is active in their lives, such conversations become testimony which can have a profound impact on others.

Finally, the community builder needs to recognize the art of humility. Young people in youth groups as communities of practice learn by talking to one another and by quizzing their leaders, have their own experience of God that gives them hope and have often worked through complex problems and dilemmas. Of course, they also have unresolved issues, make spurious decisions and can hold false assumptions about faith and life. Humility in this context not only means recognition that we don't have all the answers, but that often young people have found answers themselves. This is an important quality for leading an intentional Christian community, since it recognizes that it is the community that is active in working out what it means to be Christian, not just the leader. To be a missionary, educator or pastor in this context is to work to guide and support young people to wrestle with and work out the solutions to the questions they have and the problems they face.

For these reasons youth work works well to foster intentional Christian community. Youth work takes seriously the need for people to act on solutions that they not only understand but own, to reflect upon and share their experiences and to look to learn from those of others. Youth groups provide a community within which an ongoing participation stimulates, supports and sustains young people in forming and expressing faith. These are places that are evolving Christian presence in the world, whether they are built around 'open' or church-based provision. Within such places young people can explore their own faith identity and experience the presence of God in supportive friendships, creative worship, personal prayer and many ways we haven't yet noticed or asked about.

Questions for reflection

- Do you think of your youth group or project as a community?
- How might your church begin to 'establish Christian presence' in the world of young people where you live?
- What does young people's participation in youth work mean to you?
- In what ways can you celebrate your youth work as hospitable, honest and humble?

References and further reading

Bass, D. C. and Richter, D. C., 2002. *Way to Live: Christian practices for teens* Nashville, Upper Room Books. An American book which explores how Christian practices (prayer, worship, Sabbath) can be re-imagined with young people to help them to make space for God in their lives.

Borgman, D., 1997. *When Kumbaya Is Not Enough: A practical theology for youth ministry*. Peabody, MA, Hendrickson.

Bosch, D. J., 1991. *Transforming Mission: Paradigm shifts in theology of mission*. Maryknoll, NY, Orbis.

Dean, K. C. and Foster, R., 1998. *The Godbearing Life: The art of soul tending for youth ministry*. Nashville, Upper Room Books. A classic look at pastoral practice in youth work and how this is best set in community.

Fowler, J. W., 1999. *Becoming Christian: Adult development and Christian faith*. San Francisco, Jossey Bass.

Gardner, J., 2008. *Mend the Gap: Can the Church reconnect the generations?* Nottingham, IVP.

Graham, E. L., 1996. *Transforming Practice: Pastoral theology in an age of uncertainty*. London, Mowbray.

Green, D. E. and Green, M., 2000. *Taking a Part: Young people's participation in the Church*, edited by the Church of England Board of Education and the National Society. London, National Society/Church House Publishing.

Grenz, S. J., 1994. *Theology for the Community of God*. Carlisle, Paternoster.

Lave, J. and Wenger, E., 1991. *Situated Learning: Legitimate peripheral participation. Learning in doing: social, cognitive, and computational perspectives*. Cambridge, Cambridge University Press.

MacLaren, D., 2004. *Mission Implausible*. Carlisle, Paternoster.

Nash, S., Collins-Mayo, S. and Mayo, B., 2007. 'Raising Christian consciousness: creating place', *Journal of Youth and Theology* 6(2): 41–59.

Packham, C., 2008. *Active Citizenship and Community Learning*. Exeter, Learning Matters.

Pohl, C. D., 1999. *Making Room: Recovering hospitality as a Christian tradition*. Grand Rapids, MI, Eerdmans.

Root, A., 2007. *Revisiting Relational Youth Ministry: From strategy of influence to a theology of incarnation*. Downers Grove, IVP. Examines how sharing in young people's lives and sharing our lives with them makes space for God's presence to be known.

Savage, S. B., Collins, S. and Mayo, B., 2006. *Making Sense of Generation Y: The world view of 15- to 25-year-olds. Explorations*. London, Church House Publishing.

Shepherd, N. M., 2010. 'Christian youth groups as site for identity work', in S. Collins-Mayo and P. Dandelion (eds) *Religion and Youth*. Farnham, Ashgate.

Sofield, L., Hammett, R. and Juliano, C., 1998. *Building Community: Christian, caring, vital*. Notre Dame, IN, Ave Maria Press.

Sudworth, T., Cray, G. and Russell, C., 2007. *Mission-shaped Youth: Rethinking young people and church*. London, Church House Publishing. An exploration of how missional thinking has been adapted from and in turn developed Christian youth work

Westerhoff, J. H., 2009. *Will Our Children Have Faith?* revised edition. Chicago, Thomas More Press.

Young, K., 2006. *The Art of Youth Work*, second edition. Lyme Regis, Russell House Publishing.

5

Empowering liberator

BOB MAYO

When Nike says, just do it, that's a message of empowerment. Why aren't the rest of us speaking to young people in a voice of inspiration?   (Naomi Klein)

Setting the scene

This chapter argues that informal educators need to concern themselves with the character and not simply the decisions of a young person: good characters make good choices, and if an informal educator is able to build up the former the latter will be enabled. This chapter will also argue that just as people's characters decide their choices, so the beliefs, traditions and values of the community of which they are a part shape their characters. When the character is equipped to participate in the wider community, the work of the informal educator is done. There are three key terms used in this chapter: 'informal education', which can be defined as 'a reflective exercise which enables young people to learn from their experience, develop their capacity to think critically and engage in "sense-making" as a process of continuous self discovery and re-creation' (Young

1999: 81); 'empowerment' (character formation); and 'liberation' (community development).

The professional background to this decision to focus my educational energy on supporting a young person's character development was the move that I made from teaching youth work as the Cambridge CYM Course Director to working in a church as the vicar of St Stephen's in Shepherd's Bush. The move from youth work trainer to vicar was a change from a theoretician's to a practitioner's role. It meant a change from the social sciences to theology as my guiding discipline. It meant that I spent more time than previously in long-term one-to-one mentoring roles. I will look in detail at one such relationship and draw out the themes of character formation and community involvement, which have interested me.

The chance to have more time with fewer people freed me from the constraints imposed by previous jobs that offered less regular contact with young people. The extra time that I was able to spend with people gave me the opportunity to explore with them why they might take a decision, and the 'why' question is one more of character than of choice. The question was less 'Is it wrong?' or 'Is it right?' and more 'What does it mean? Is it the person you wish to become . . . ? Does the person you see yourself to be behave in this way?'

Helping someone to decide on what sort of person he or she wants to be is primarily an ethical activity, and therein lay the new territory that I was beginning to occupy. My new professional role meant that I was clearly identified as a part of a church community and this became the context for my ethics. I am with Wells (2006: 2) in saying that 'theology and ethics are two sides of the same coin'; theological ethics is not simply a study of human action, but a discipline that works itself out through the practice and mutual accountability of community building. He suggests that 'What sustains human life is a pattern of practices – good ways to relate to one another, honed in community and developed by tradition, learned by apprenticeship and embodied in habit' (Wells 2006: 2).

Thus it was that two things had changed. I found myself more closely identified with the Church as a community of belief, and my educational role was addressing ethical identity questions. Together these gave me the impetus to widen my educational terms of reference, from simply supporting individuals in the choices they might want to make, to enabling those people to develop the character they needed in order to make good choices for themselves; therein lies the 'empowerment' of the individual.

Strategic liberalism

I would not have been so willing to shift my educational practice in this way had I not already begun to identify flaws in a youth work informal education that concentrated on decision-making to the exclusion of character development. *The Faith of Generation Y* (Collins-Mayo *et al.* 2010) was a four-year research project in which I was involved that looked at the role played by Christian youth work in heightening a young person's Christian consciousness. The book identified a conceptual muddle at the heart of youth work practice, whereby the youth workers appeared to want to adopt informal education as a method but to keep Christianity as the substance; there appeared to be a loose-fitting hope that if young people are encouraged to make choices then Christianity might be one of the decisions they make.

The Faith of Generation Y described this as 'strategic liberalism' (cf. Hauerwas 1981: 11) and argued that it unintentionally created an ethos of indifference towards Christianity. This was for two reasons. When the role of informal education was seen as largely helping young people 'critically' to reflect back on the choices they wished to make, there was a danger that the process would end up feeding back to them what they thought of as important anyhow. If choice was perpetuated as a self-validating principle then there was no reason why Christianity should be seen as anything more important than anything else, as other than a lifestyle option. It appeared that even if a young person recognized that the youth worker had a Christian faith there was still no reason for him or her to think of the youth worker as anything other than a 'nice guy'.

Empowerment

The two pillars of character and community have underpinned conversations that I have had over the last year with Ed, a final year undergraduate student. During this time he has proposed to his girlfriend, completed a course in craniosacral therapy and made a Christian commitment. We meet in a café for an hour, with him leading the questions and me responding. Among other things, we have talked about the spirituality of yoga, the Christian teaching on sexuality and, latterly, the meaning of repentance and new birth.

Our conversations are driven by Ed's desire to understand his newfound Christian faith, and his interest in Christianity has been primarily in understanding how it will help him to develop as a person. He has only secondarily known what Christianity teaches as 'right' or 'wrong' about certain issues. This is consistent with *The Faith of Generation Y*'s conclusion that young people were not interested in faith as a propositional truth but wanted to know what difference it would make to their lives. For the young people the key question was not 'Is it true?' but 'Does it work?' They want to know what a life of faith might look like in practice.

Our conversations were driven by a sense of Ed becoming the person he wanted to be. My challenge to him was not so much changed behaviour as transformed character; character produces hope (Romans 5.4) and this is the type of person I wanted him to become. What kept our conversations from becoming a theological version of 'strategic liberalism' was the fact that they were anchored in the Church as the holder of the Christian story. Our conversations were shaped round the central theological concept of us being made in God's image. I return to this later.

Wright (2010: 33) suggests that my interest in character transformation taps into a tradition of moral thinking that goes back to Aristotle. He writes that it was Aristotle, about 350 years before the time of Jesus, who developed the threefold pattern of character transformation. There is first the goal; this is the person that Ed would like to become. There are then the steps Ed would need to take towards this 'goal': these are the qualities (virtues) that he would need to demonstrate in order to become such a person. Finally there are the repeated patterns of behaviour and moral training through which these qualities (virtues) turn into habits, becoming second nature and a natural part of who Ed is in the society.

For the period of our exploratory conversations together, a primary virtue was wisdom, primarily because this shaped the purpose for which we were meeting. Ed was beginning the process of learning how to run together his own story with the Christian narrative. He was reconsidering how he lived his life while not wanting to change the structures to what he did; he was very committed to his course and to his girlfriend (now fiancée). Herein began the educational dialogue between the two of us; the theme of empowerment through dialogue is echoed by Taylor's comment on Paulo Freire's work: 'The Christian truth is dialogical; it is loving, humble, hopeful, trusting and critical. It emerges out of the interaction between different perspectives within the same situation' (1993: 62).

I was inducting Ed into a tradition of thought (Scripture) and offering him an invitation to be a part of a community (Church). This is the classic discipleship role. Hauerwas talks of the Church as 'a community capable of forming people with virtues [faith, hope and love (1 Corinthians 13)] sufficient to witness to God's truth in the world'(1981: 84). In this sense the role of the Christian community was twofold. It embodied the reality of what I was telling Ed about the Christian faith and it provided a narrative through which he could make sense of his life.

The Faith of Generation Y found that the young people were not going to understand what they were hearing about the Christian faith, unless there was (some form of) community of believers to embody the story. Young people were not going to absorb what they heard of the Christian faith unless they were in some way connected with some form of Christian community (even if this was a residual sense of identification from their childhood). They were not going to be able to process free-floating bits of information when they did not have a context in which they could place what they were hearing.

Hauerwas wrote: 'The Scriptures tell the story of the forgiving love of God and the church is an extended argument over time about the significance of that story and how to interpret it' (1981: 383). When the Scriptures are not interpreted through the lenses of the Church, people think falsely in terms of 'back to the Bible' in order to create a purist understanding of Scripture. When Scripture is used to shape the Church and the Church is equipped to make sense of Scripture, we create an eschatological dynamic whereby we can talk of forward (rather than back) to the Bible. Ed wants to explore a narrative that provides a sufficiently coherent account of his existence and he will find this embodied in the life of the church community.

Narratives

Mayo *et al.* (2004) wrote that a 'narrative' model of self is one in which we develop into the person we are to become through the developing 'story' of our life experience. In the quest to make sense of our personal lives and the world around, people are dependent on narratives that provide the plot by means of which we tell the story of our lives. The community that embodies the narrative mediates the overarching meaning to the individual person. Ed's exploring a Christian faith means that he is learning to tell his personal story and to find an identity in accordance with a particular narrative, the story which has been passed from generation to generation through the church community but which is ultimately found in the Bible, the book of the community. It is through the telling of stories that we come to know who we are and what life is about for us.

I am introducing Ed to a Christian narrative of truth and need to have a clear conception of what this is. The Christian concept of truth is so gentle that it does not break a bruised reed (Isaiah 42.3) but at the same time it is sharp and incisive enough to judge the thoughts and attitudes of the heart (Hebrews 4.12). The spiritual person makes judgements (i.e. discernment) in everything (1 Corinthians 2.15) but does not condemn people (Matthew 7.1). Jesus was both discursive to the woman caught in adultery and dogmatic to her accusers (John 8.4). Drawing in the sand while they waited for him to speak was a practical way of taking the heat out of the situation and a figurative way of showing his own feelings – figures in the sand can be reshaped in the same way that ideas can be revised and that was what he was wanting the woman's accusers to do. When he sees that they are implacable, he breaks his silence and tells those without sin to cast the first stone.

This theological framing of truth emerges from the combination of the two Old Testament images for the Messiah. The gentleness of truth comes out of the image of the suffering servant of Isaiah (53) and the sharpness of truth comes out of the powerful image of the Son of Man of Daniel (7). This is developed in the New Testament, where the gentleness emerges from the grace and the sharpness from the majesty of God. The twin ideas of majesty and grace then provide the backdrop for understanding sin and forgiveness. To focus on the concepts of human sin, responsibility and guilt without simultaneously having confidence in the divine work of atonement undercuts the gentle, creative and illuminating nature of Christian judgement. It is diagnosis without prescription (Stott 1989).

Our conversations will draw to a natural conclusion as Ed becomes absorbed into the wider Christian community. He is now considering the possibility of being baptized and of going on an Alpha course to formalize the learning that we have done together. It is significant that it is in the process of making this transition from individual conversations to membership of the wider community that Ed has absorbed some of the more overtly Christian concepts, such as repentance and rebirth.

Liberation

The principal virtues of the Christian faith are the fruit of the spirit: love, joy, peace, longsuffering, kindness, goodness, faithfulness, gentleness, self-control (Galatians 5.22). The fruit of the spirit is experienced through participation in the wider Christian community. It is an involvement in the church community that will take Ed's learning about the Christian faith on beyond anything that he and I can learn together. A progressive decline in church attendance has weakened people's confidence in the Church as an agent of revelation. There has also been a tendency within the family of informal education to distance itself from the church community. I would argue that this is a way of establishing a separate professional identity rather than valid educational methodology. *The Faith of Generation Y* found that as the Church we needed to have confidence in who we were, be our authentic selves.

It is not just theology but also science that requires a community of knowledge in order to be able to establish learning. Polanyi (1983) establishes that, just as Ed needs the community of the Church to learn the Christian story, a scientist in pursuit of knowledge needs the wider scientific community. The scientist is not an isolated individual unaffected by the rules, directions and discoveries of the wider scientific community. The scientific community provides both a point of reference and also a definition of task to the scientist. Just as with Ed in his voyage of discovery, it is an active participation rather than a passive presence that defines a person as a member of the scientific community; in Polanyi's terms, being is doing (Polanyi 1983: 379). The role of science is akin to the role of the Church in that it imposes a framework of discipline at the same time as encouraging rebellion against it. The role of the scientist is to learn from, grow through and then challenge the teaching of the scientific community. For both scientist and the theologian, learning comes through the community of which they are a part.

The mutual interaction of learning through a community is reflected in the idea that God created us in his own image (Genesis 1.27). Being made in the image of God does not mean individual enlightenment but rather community learning. Grenz (2001) argues that the image of God is a social rather than an individual reality – it is a way of relating to other people rather than the Gnostic idea that there is a spark of light hidden deep within us. The biblical focus is on 'we' being the divine image rather than the image being lodged within each individual. The *imago dei* is a communal concept. The locus of the divine image in the New Testament is the community of Christ rather than the individual believer. It is this reality that is now opening up for Ed.

Postscript

The idea of 'character' and 'choices' has become a recurring theme within my church since the Hoosiers released a single entitled 'Stop giving me choices'; Sam, the organist at the church, is the keyboard player in the band. The song talks about how young people struggle to deal with the multiple-choice approach to community living that society offers. There is pressure on them and they can sometimes find it hard to cope. My suggestion in this chapter is that the answer to too many choices is character and community.

Questions for reflection

- How might you help young people to identify the ideal self that they would like themselves to be?
- What are the primary learning communities to which the young people belong?
- How can the informal educator work alongside these communities to help young people identify possible life choices?
- How do we facilitate young people engaging with the biblical story and church community?

References and further reading

Collins-Mayo, S., Mayo, B., Nash, S. and Cocksworth, C., 2010. *The Faith of Generation Y*. London, Church House Publishing, 2010. Contemporary research with strong theological and theoretical underpinning to help you work effectively with this group.

Grenz, S., 2001. *The Social God and the Relational Self: A Trinitarian theology of the imago dei*. Louisville, KY, Westminster John Knox Press.

Hauerwas, S., 1981. *A Community of Character*. Notre Dame, University of Notre Dame Press.

Mayo, B., Collins, S. and Savage, S., 2004. *Ambiguous Evangelism*. London, SPCK. Helps you explore evangelism with unchurched young people.

Polanyi, M., 1983. *Personal Knowledge: Towards a post-critical philosophy*. London, Routledge and Kegan Paul; first published in 1958.

Stott, J., 1989. *The Cross of Christ*. Leicester, IVP.

Taylor, P., 1993. *The Texts of Paulo Freire*. Buckingham, Open University Press.

Wells, S., 2006. *God's Companions – Reimagining Christian Ethics*. Oxford, Blackwell.

Wright, N. T., 2010. *After You Believe*. London, HarperCollins. Exploration of virtue and the importance of Christian character.

Young, K., 1999. *The Art of Youth Work*. Lyme Regis, Russell House Publishing. Good introduction to youth work from a philosophical perspective.

6

Party planner

JEAN HARPER

Yeah they make it much fun, like if they weren't here we'd just be talking to everybody, and you'd think well my mates are having much better time than I am and I might as well get in trouble with them and get a buzz out of that, but they make . . . the environment much better.

(Barry's response in an interview by
a researcher of Christian youth work)

Setting the scene

Up and down the land on New Year's Eve 1999 churches were holding parties to celebrate the new millennium. For some people this meant not having to celebrate on their own – they could be part of a community, a family. Children and the elderly happily mixed together, people shared food, games, dancing, fireworks, experiences that could be remembered and stories that could be told and retold. Together many of us celebrated two thousand years of Christian history. For many, church was experienced as fun and inclusive.

Party planner may not be a role you initially think of as a youth minister, but we think it is essential for holistic youth ministry. It is so easy to get into a rut, but sometimes we need to make an opportunity to celebrate, to rejoice in the lives of individual young people, the festivals of the Christian year and wider cultural events. Let's do Christmas in July for someone who was in hospital in December, or celebrate some small achievement of a young person who is rarely the centre of attention, or have a sleepover on the longest day of the year. There are so many opportunities to celebrate and party if we just look for them.

However, celebration in this way is not always the experience of young people. Consider the non-linear story that Quentin Tarantino used in the film *Pulp Fiction* to depict the life and times of drug-dealing war lords. How far away it seemed from the reality of our lives, yet now this blend of humour and violence has become common. Such images soften the impact of news bulletins that tell us that numerous young people have chosen to follow a pathway of destruction or have fallen victim to another in pursuit of fun, fame, financial gain, excitement, new opportunities and all the excess life has to offer. How do we break into this narrative to introduce young people to the thrill of knowing and serving our creator God, to the transformational potential of the gospel and the sense of belonging we can experience as part of the family of God?

To be creative and effective, youth workers need to know the young people they have chosen to serve. We must also be reflective to ensure that the flavour of the provision changes with the needs and type of young people with whom we come into contact. Church must be more influential, inspiring and consistently godly. In the Acts of the Apostles we see how the lives of the individuals spoke to those around them and gave witness to the quality of life worshipping God offers.

'I came that they may have life, and have it abundantly,' said Jesus (John 10.10). The promise of life may seem to be no big pull, but the story of the ordinary carpenter's boy invites and engages young people in a dialogue that challenges and changes lives. Young people want it all and they want it now. Living on the edge, getting the next buzz, taking things to another level is all part of our now world. These tensions provide the much needed thrust to be outstanding for God – living a life that is full of seeking God's will for now, serving the young people and their community, and following in God's lead by modelling and reflecting upon the reality of knowing and celebrating God personally. It may also involve us mediating with the wider Church and helping its members to understand the cultural context young people live in today, with the pressures and issues they face, and why sometimes what we see and hear seems to be in conflict with their expressed faith.

Traditional youth work demonstrates one way of celebrating. Within local authority youth work the celebration of outcomes is encouraged – Youth Achievement Awards, certificates, party events, newspaper articles, trips, vouchers and the like. Ideally these acknowledgements are planned with a small group of young people to ensure relevance. They understand that by working towards a planned outcome the group will receive its chosen reward. Any opportunity for learning new skills cannot be overlooked or undercelebrated. Girls' and Boys' Brigades, are among the uniformed organizations that encourage young people to celebrate their ability and the learning of new skills on a more regular basis. Young people come to understand that by working consistently to develop their knowledge, attitudes and skills, they will be rewarded by their effort and given a badge or certificate as well as the acknowledgement of their peers. These organizations have helped to develop competitive, determined, community-minded and self-aware young people. Church-based and faith groups offer the experience of incarnation, the fifth pillar of youth work that Brierley (2003) speaks of. Commendably they place parties, celebrations and tributes within a structured environment that is not embarrassed to put Jesus at the centre.

Research suggests that such activities are good for young people: 'Young people who are members of youth/sports clubs are better citizens' and 'Young people who are members of clubs feel valued and valuable' (nfpSynergy on behalf of the Scout Association 2007: 3–4). Encouragingly for us as youth workers, this same research found that 'Youth group leaders [are] a stronger influence than the neighbourhood' (2007: 9). This, along with young people's desire to have fun and enjoy their activities, suggests that the role of party planner is an important one for a youth worker, as that attitude or motivation helps create the environment that attracts young people to our youth work and gives church young people some confidence in inviting their friends to activities as well. In the rest of this chapter we will explore both larger celebration 'party'-type events and the weekly activities that are at the heart of most youth ministry.

Planning a celebration event for and with young people

It is vital to understand the benefits of creating celebration events: they can provide an impetus for community building, for young people to contribute their ideas and gifts, and to help promote the idea that Christianity is a joyful life-giving religion that has something to offer the pursuit of happiness that seems to be the motivation for many young people (Savage *et al.* 2006). Celebration is also something that deeply resonates with the biblical narrative, and indeed, introducing young people to some of the key events and festivals of our faith is a way in which we can communicate the Christian story in engaging and accessible ways.

Get young people involved

Talking with the young people about their ideas for the celebration is a step towards participation; engaging them in the development of these ideas to the point where an event takes place is an empowering process. Young people want to be listened to. Being part of making something happen can boost their confidence and esteem as well as developing their awareness of the needs of others. Such outcomes align with the government's 'Every Child Matters' agenda. We need to consider how we shape young people as we advocate, support and assist them to think through ideas purposefully. We need to be aware of the tension between having fun yet ensuring that Christ is honoured; stories of his life show that he was not afraid to party even at the risk of being misunderstood.

When working with a group to explore the purpose of the celebration, use words like 'aim' to draw out what they perceive to be the work in hand. Ask them what they want to achieve, how they would like to feel at the end of the event, what they want the outcomes to be. It is important also to foster ownership – you may not get 100 per cent agreement, but in order for the group's work to proceed young people will need to understand compromise and how to foster the ideas of others so that the celebration is the focus, not individual flair or preferences.

Hart's (1992) ladder of participation is a useful model to consider as we seek to get young people involved and try to move up the rungs if our starting point is not where we want to be:

8 Young people initiate and share decisions with adults – young people are empowered but have the opportunity to learn from adults.

7 Young people initiate and are directed – adults support.

6 Adults initiate and share decisions with young people.

5 Young people are consulted and informed.

4 Young people are assigned roles but informed about their involvement.

The next three rungs are non-participation so to be avoided.

3 Tokenism: young people appear to have a voice but little notice is taken in reality.

2 Decoration: young people are used to help the cause but indirectly.

1 Manipulation: young people are used to support causes but adults may pretend causes were inspired by the young people.

Event suggestions

These are some tried and tested ideas that work well for celebrations:

- roller disco, Christmas Ball (or other seasonal events);
- rites of passage;
- summer café, afternoon tea, breakfast events;
- events in the Bible or church tradition: Passover meal, foot-washing, Ash Wednesday service, New Year's Eve watchnight party and service, etc.;
- praise party, gigs, speakers or comedy events;
- fashion showcase;
- TV-themed events (*Come Dine with Me, Young Apprentice, We've All Got Talent, The X Factor* . . .);
- monthly youth service;
- fund-raising events.

Ask young people what they would like to do. Think what works well intergenerationally, party with a purpose, be clear as to what you want to achieve.

Getting support and planning

You will want to involve and get support from the wider church, and this may include: money, buildings and equipment (check insurance), prayer, sponsorship from members, specific talents and skills, publicity, tuck shop help, lifts, prayer ministry or bouncers! You may also want to consider whether there are other sources of funding. You could look at voluntary sector grants, the Youth Opportunity Fund or local trusts. There will often be a voluntary services group or staff at a denominational or local authority level who can help you with where to look. Sponsorship from local businesses is another possibility, including donations of food, prizes, printing of publicity or even staff help. If you are going to be doing an open community event you need to make the police aware and invite them, as well as informing neighbours and others who may be impacted by the event.

It is vital to complete all the paperwork and plan thoroughly and in good time. Again, young people can be involved in this. Consider risk assessments, leader participant ratios, safeguarding policies, health and safety, including a building check list, bouncers, a first-aider, etc., access and disability issues, insurance, licences, food hygiene, contingency plans, budgeting, setting up and clearing up.

Evaluating the event

Ask such questions as:

- How did the event come about?
- Who took the lead in the event?
- How were young people involved? What were their roles and responsibilities?
- What happened on the night? Who made the decisions?
- What training and ministry development was involved?
- Did we achieve the aims, objectives, planned outcomes? (important for funders)
- What were the challenges of the event?
- How did you evaluate and with whom?
- Who wrote the report?
- What were the outcomes for the young people?
- How can the event be followed up with ongoing skill development and nurture?
- What can we learn for next time?

Programme planning

Along with celebrations we need to consider the regular programmes we run. Here we are looking to combine enjoyment and fun with informal education. Part of the educational value may well be the young people taking responsibility for helping to shape the programme and putting it together – participation in the youth work sense of the word. Chapter 9, 'Guardian of souls', discusses spiritual and faith development which will be a part of what we want to do with our programmes, but in considering a holistic approach to development we also need to think about the cognitive, emotional and social strands (Thompson 2004). There is usually an educational part to our programmes and thus the cognitive strand will normally be addressed. Emotions are part of the strategy we have for dealing with the outside world and responding to things that happen to us. It can be beneficial to be aware of our own emotions and how they impact the way that we do youth work, but also to be sensitive to the emotions of the young people we work with and, perhaps particularly, to help them learn how to handle and process negative emotions such as fear, anger, guilt and shame. We partly do this by modelling, but it may also be helpful to do some specific teaching on such topics. The Bible provides us with rich resources for this, as well as the breadth of popular culture. Also, we should seek to facilitate young people experiencing positive emotions such as joy, hope, peace, love and wonder.

With regard to social development there are four key areas to consider:

- moral – learning right from wrong, transmission of cultural norms and values;
- interpersonal – relating to others, social skills, behaviour;
- social location – class, race and culture, gender, age, disability and so on;
- political – power, rights, freedom from abuse (Thompson 2004: 27).

Again, these can be underlying objectives in our programmes or at times the main focus of what we are doing. We must be real about the challenges and pressures our young people face and discuss openly with them such topics as sex, drugs, self-harm and bullying – our curriculum needs to be rooted in their experience as well as in the Bible. We hope for young people to experience life in all its fullness, and part of what we need to do to enable this is to give them the tools they need to make the most of the opportunities open to them, as well as inviting them to get to know Jesus and giving them the opportunity to respond to the gospel message.

Merton and Wylie articulate a pedagogy (approach to teaching) for youth work which includes project- and activity-led learning that is relevant and interesting; negotiates terms and conditions with the young people; specifies outcomes; recognizes and stimulates different forms of intelligence – the emotional as well as the intellectual; works with groups and different individuals; blends challenges and skills at the right level – too much is intimidating, too little is boring; and offers effective support, mentoring and brokering to underpin learning (2002: 11). Chapter 5, 'Empowering liberator', also talks about how we approach learning with young people, and it is important that we work out our own approach to running our youth work. Lambert (2004) lists the tasks of Christian teachers in a youth ministry context:

- Teach what God's Word says (Exodus 18.20).
- Be an example of how to live (Titus 2.7).
- Teach others how to obey God (Matthew 28.20).
- Teach the younger generations (Deuteronomy 4.9).
- Teach all the time, not just in class (Acts 5.42).
- Teach non-Christians so they will come to know God (Acts 17.19–20).
- Bring out new treasures as well as old (Matthew 13.52).
- Stir people up (Luke 23.5).
- Prepare others to do something for the kingdom of God (Ephesians 4.11–12).
- Help make believers complete (Colossians 1.28).
- Confront false teaching (2 Timothy 1.13).
- Look for others who will make great leaders and teachers (2 Timothy 2.2).

This helps give us a biblical context for our role and inspires us as to the range of tasks we can undertake. It may also be the case that people in our youth ministry team have different giftings and feel more drawn to particular elements.

Curriculum

One of the things you may want to do is put together a curriculum – a termly or annual plan for what you want your young people to learn. Generally with a curriculum you would have learning outcomes –

what you want young people to be able to know and understand, feel or do at the end of the session – a pedagogy as discussed above and how you might evaluate what you have done. This list, adapted from Lambert (2004: 122) is helpful in drawing up our learning outcomes:

- Know: arrange, define, list, memorize, name, order, recognize, relate, recall, repeat, state, classify, describe, explain, express, identify, indicate, locate, report, review, select.
- Feel: accept, challenge, defend, dispute, judge, question, share, support, have confidence, be convicted, wonder, experience, own, embrace.
- Do: apply, choose, demonstrate, employ, illustrate, interpret, practice, schedule, solve, use, write, analyse, appraise, categorize, compare, contrast, criticize, distinguish, examine, experiment, question, test, arrange, assemble, compose, construct, create, design, develop, formulate, manage, organize, plan, prepare, propose, serve, help, assist.

Problems

Thus far we have explored assessing the needs of our young people, considering a curriculum and setting appropriate learning outcomes. We now need to identify appropriate activities and put together a programme. Chapter 7, 'Boundary marker', discusses how we manage behaviour in groups once we are underway with our activities. Benson (2000) offers some suggestions as to why programmes and activities do not always work:

- There has been a failure to base the programme on identified group and individual need and relate it to outcomes.
- The programme content or outcomes are unrealistic.
- The programme is too rigid and doesn't give the opportunity to build on spontaneous and unexpected incidents and events, which may mean that we miss some of the fun.
- There is not enough balance between the needs of the person and the requirements of the task; this can include activities above or below the group's level.
- There is a poor or inappropriate selection of activity.
- The activity becomes an end in itself rather than a means of learning.
- There has been a failure to evaluate and review the programme.

Regular team planning meetings and a debrief after each event or session help mitigate against some of these problems. Finding ways for young people to feed back honestly is always helpful, particularly at the beginning of the planning process. We also need to be comfortable in discussing issues with young people, helping them explore their choices and supporting them even when they make choices that are not in line with ours. We need to try and see the world through the eyes of our young people; for some of us this can be difficult as their world and experience is so very different from ours when we were their age. We may also need to advocate on behalf of the young people and the youth work – party planner may not be the role church leaders see us in, and we need to be wary of compromising our God-given vision to accommodate others.

Conclusion

Being a party planner means taking account of our creativity, our desire to play, to have fun, to laugh and learn together. But it is not an alternative to taking the gospel and our role as youth workers seriously and wanting to see young people's lives transformed. Berard *et al.* (2010: 71) offer these challenges to us as we seek to develop our ministry with young people:

- youth independence: commitment to youth independence and the right to theological vocation, joyful service and good accommodation within our faith community;
- youth influence: genuine opportunity for youth influence and participation in the community at large;
- youth resource: youth commitment, creativity and critical thinking viewed as resources.

Let's point the way for young people to life in all its fullness and help them to see that Christianity offers the fun, pleasure and joy that they look for elsewhere, while also introducing them to a holistic gospel that is challenging, transformational and life-changing. 'For we are what he has made us, created in Christ Jesus for good works, which God prepared beforehand to be our way of life' (Ephesians 2.10). Is party planner part of that for you?

Questions for reflection

- What is your response to the idea of being a party planner?
- How can you incorporate more celebration into your programme?
- Which of the rungs of Hart's ladder are you currently on? Where would you like to be?
- What are your strengths and weaknesses in programme planning?

References and further reading

Benson, J. F., 2000. *Working More Creatively with Small Groups*, second edition. London, Routledge.

Berard, J., Penner, J. and Bartlett, R., 2010. *Consuming Youth*. Grand Rapids, MI, Zondervan. A robust challenge to re-imagine youth ministry in a way that engages young people and offer an alternative way of living to our consumer culture.

Brierley, D., 2003. *Joined Up. An introduction to youthwork and ministry*. London, Authentic. Now out of print, but if you can track down a copy it will help you to understand what good practice is, from both perspectives.

Hart, R., 1992. *Children's Participation from Tokenism to Citizenship*. Florence, UNICEF.

Lambert, D., 2004. *Teaching that Makes a Difference*. Grand Rapids, MI, Zondervan. A comprehensive introduction to teaching in a Christian context – challenges you to think through what you do.

Merton, B. and Wylie, T., 2002. *Towards a Contemporary Curriculum for Youth Work*. Leicester, National Youth Agency.

nfpSynergy, 2007. *Typical Young People – A study of what young people are really like today*. Report commissioned by the Scout Association, available at <www.nfpsynergy.net/includes/documents/cm_docs/2008/t/typical_young_people.pdf>.

Savage, S., Collins-Mayo, S., Mayo, B. and Cray, G., 2006. *Making Sense of Generation Y*. London: Church House Publishing.

Thompson, N., 2004. *Group Care with Children and Young People*, second edition. Lyme Regis, Russell House Publishing.

7

Boundary marker

SHARON MCKIBBIN

> If the postmodern world will not take heed of the gospel message, it just might take note of the quality and sheer vitality and authenticity of the care with which the Christian community embraces a hurting and disintegrating world in the name of Christ. (Paul Goodliff)

I was cutting it close. Five minutes until the doors opened for youth club, and I was still in my office trying to fix a table tennis bat, a fatality from last week. Outside the building, young people were gathering at the door. I was two volunteers down. Then I saw him. Putting my head around the door, I called, 'Griff, remember you're banned this week,' noticing the cigarette butts at his feet and decimated tulip heads behind him. 'They should be dovetailed like spoons in a drawer,' the caretaker had reminded me *again* this morning, referring to the fold-down tables in the cupboard I'd used the night before. Last week it was a stash of empty crisp packets behind the Coke machine. Wait until he sees the tulips, I thought.

Griff looked up. Greasy hair, earphones and new trainers. 'Why?' he simply asked.

Here we go, I thought. Pointing to a brand new pool cue: 'Remember last week, when you . . .'

On Sunday, the Senior Pastor had thanked me for the work I did with the youth. He was genuine, but thinking about leading the youth work team stressed me. Some local youth had broken three windows and disrupted two Sunday services recently; an appropriate response was causing division within the volunteer team.

Griff kicked the door, 'NO! This is a church, you can't f***ing ban me.'

'I'm sorry but *you are* banned. You know the rules, I'll see you next—'

'I wanna become a Christian,' he interjected, his voice changed.

I sighed. This tactic worked on some volunteers. 'Mate, I don't have time for this right now. I'm sorry, come back next week,' I said as I closed the door.

I became a youth and community worker because I wanted to make a difference to the lives of young people, in the same way as my life had been changed through relationships with Christian youth workers. I dreamt of opportunities to change families and transform communities. However, I learnt the hard way at the beginning of my career. I was too busy, balancing two youth work jobs and my degree. At times I was putting on a mask to do the job, was neglecting my own personal relationship with God and living far away from support structures of friends and family. I wasn't confident responding to young people who were challenging, at managing difference of opinion among volunteers or creatively leading an under-resourced youth group. Truthfully, I felt dishonest when church leaders encouraged me in my role because I sometimes wanted young people like Griff to go away.

Being a boundary marker

Beginning in Genesis 12, God invited Abraham and his descendants to move to the promised land in Canaan. Later, in Genesis 15, God confirmed the unconditional nature of the covenant. God also established his authority through guidelines and boundaries with the Israelites in the form of the Ten Commandments, and the books of Leviticus and Deuteronomy. Throughout the Old Testament, it is clear that when the Israelites followed the guidelines they experienced blessing, but equally experienced God's condemnation when they were disobedient. However, these boundaries and instructions given by God were independent of his covenant, promise and uncon-ditional love. In the same way, youth workers offer young people relationships, significance and belonging, but with boundaries and consequences. A clear tension exists between young people dis-regarding rules and behaviour and the potential risk of losing relationships with leaders and access to activities. Therefore, it is vital young people know that our relationships with them are unconditional.

While there are some examples of boundaries being damaging or violating human dignity (e.g. Palestine, apartheid in South Africa, Catholic and Protestant conflict in Northern Ireland) boundaries can provide freedom and security. Take driving, for example: while it is frustrating to receive a parking ticket, there would be chaos if all car drivers were able to park anywhere. Equally, other transport-related boundaries such as driving on the left side of the road bring freedom to all road users. Similarly, the boundaries God gave to the Israelites and rules created by youth workers exist for the benefit of everyone involved.

Any relationship involves establishing and maintaining bound-aries. In youth work, these are professional, ethical and behavioural. In recognizing and maintaining professional boundaries as a youth worker, we ensure young people are free from oppression and live safely. For example, youth work should not be confused with friendship, though a youth worker adopts a strategy of being friendly with a young person to build a relationship. Therefore, ethically youth workers shouldn't date young people or act in any way that might suggest that. In establishing and policing behav-ioural boundaries among young people, such as violence and bullying, we are helping young people learn appropriate behav-iour with their peers, promoting interdependence and community through intentional activities and, ultimately, preparing them for adulthood.

That one youth worker might challenge an ungrateful attitude in comparison to another is due to values. Values come from our own life experience, our own personal understanding of God and from within the youth work profession. However, there are a set of values that are central to the youth work profession that mark the territory. In Northern Ireland, the Model for Effective Practice outlines equity (promoting equality of opportunity), diversity (recognizing and celebrating diversity) and interdependence (building interdependent relationships) as values that should underpin work with young people. In England, youth work has been shaped by the values of voluntary participation, informal education, empowerment and equality of opportunity.

Facilitation skills

Good facilitation skills are core to being an effective boundary marker. Facilitation is the process of assisting a group to accomplish a task. It involves helping a group to gel, identify problems and resolve conflict. The facilitator remains objective and will deliberately not take too much control of the group, asking questions to encourage reflection and deeper self-awareness. He or she will also use a range of strategies to encourage participation by all. Cameron (2005: 4) presents three scales, shown in Table 7.1, which will aid the youth worker's reflection in identifying positives and negatives in our preferred facilitation styles.

Table 7.1 Preferred facilitation style

ACTIVE	*REFLECTIVE*
Enthusiastic (+)	Thoughtful (+)
Stimulating (+)	Gives people time (+)
Talks too much (−)	Pace too slow (−)
Gives own opinions (−)	Too much silence (−)
THEORETICAL	*FACT-BASED*
Creative (+)	Practical (+)
Builds on ideas for the future (+)	Strong on solving problems (+)
Not pragmatic (−)	May not value creative ideas (−)
May be seen as woolly by participants (−)	May not look ahead (−)
AGGRESSIVE	*PASSIVE*
Time managed well (+)	Group has a feeling of control (+)
Pre-defined topics covered (+)	Lots of flexibility in the discussion (+)
Little flexibility in discussion topics (−)	Weak controls on time (−)
Highly directive (−)	Not directive at all – can seem aimless (−)

Be prepared

When facilitating, always have a plan and never promise what you cannot deliver. This will involve developing a programme in advance, in consultation with young people, that is relevant and interesting to them (see Chapter 6, 'Party planner'). Either develop your own or visit your local Christian bookshop for small group programmes that are ready to go and look to adapt them for your group. Remember to delegate tasks to other volunteers and possibly young people in the group, which will take the weekly pressure off you. On the night, leave plenty of time to set up the room and prepare activities, ensuring you are not rushed or stressed before you start. Also, do not run over time as parents will be expecting young people home at a certain time or waiting outside in the car, but do plan to have a debrief with your team so you can learn for next time.

Care for physical needs

Take into consideration physical needs such as refreshments. Is the seating comfortable? Is the temperature of the room too warm? Do new young people know where the toilet is? Are there any distracting noises from outside the room?

Create and maintain an open environment

A group will flourish when young people feel comfortable sharing their ideas. Youth workers should encourage young people to listen to each other by using creative and non-threatening activities such as carefully planned ice-breakers. Also be aware of signs that indicate young people are not involved, such as body language and level of participation.

Lead by example

Enhance the dynamics of the group by being open, punctual and respectful. Being warm and friendly in attitude, words and body language will help young people feel accepted. In addition, ensure that you always participate in the activities even when you are not facilitating. You cannot expect young people to do something (e.g. an ice-breaker) that you are not prepared to do yourself. Last, ask a more experienced facilitator to observe and give you feedback.

Devise a contract with the group

Working with the group to devise a contract or a set of rules will increase ownership. General principles in the contract might include the importance of punctuality, equal participation, listening to each other, confidentiality, openness and sensitivity.

Challenging behaviour

Challenging behaviour is any behaviour that disrupts youth work activities and their enjoyment and that is a concern to other young people or to the youth worker. It may range from not following instructions and breaking rules to bullying, verbal abuse, aggression, violence and damage to property. It is a common belief that the disciples were teenagers during Jesus' ministry. Therefore, when you read the Gospels, imagine Griff or a young person you know walking, living and being with Jesus every day. The disciples displayed behaviour that was violent (Peter cut off a soldier's ear in Luke 22.49–51) and threatening (suggesting to Jesus that 'fire from heaven' should incinerate the Samaritans in Luke 9.54 after they are snubbed). They also frequently didn't listen, as illustrated when Jesus told them he would die and come back to life (John 12.23–34; Matthew 17.9; Mark 9.31–32; Luke 9.22). In Mark 10.32–34 Jesus emphasizes 'again' (v. 32b) the prediction of his death. Even the Pharisees knew Jesus would rise from the dead (Matthew 27.63) asking Pilate to make the tomb more secure (Matthew 27.65). Yet they acted as they did in brokenness and doubt when these things happened. One story in Luke 9 highlights their immaturity again, when after a number of miracles and supernatural experiences we find the disciples arguing over who would be the greatest (v. 46). In the light of all they had witnessed, they were found arguing over who would be the most famous, honoured and respected of them!

Understanding challenging behaviour

One of the key factors in managing challenging behaviour is understanding how it occurs. Sapin (2009: 132) explains the source of conflict under four headings:

Perspectives

With a perspectives conflict, young people might refuse to co-operate through a difference in value system and ideology, often strengthened by poor understanding of others. In Northern Ireland, there is often conflict between young people from Protestant and Catholic backgrounds. Youth workers can begin to disable this source of conflict by creating an inclusive environment that challenges discriminatory remarks about young people from other ethnic, religious or cultural backgrounds, and developing programmes that create opportunities to meet others from a different identity.

Interpersonal relationships

Interpersonal conflict is common as it is based on young people who dislike each other, have differing interests and a history of previous misunderstandings. It is good practice to develop a group contract at the beginning of any youth work activity with regular reminders to manage this source of conflict. It is important that activities are well planned to build in time for activities that develop relationships between young people who have interpersonal conflict.

Intrapersonal dilemma

Young people's insecurity or history of unhappy relationships with parents can cause some young people to dominate and control, or in other cases retreat within themselves. It can be a challenge to integrate domineering young people with an internal intrapersonal dilemma as they are often the fuel of fighting and arguing. It is important to work one-on-one with young people experiencing intrapersonal dilemma to identify the internal source of conflict and work towards building up personal confidence and self-belief.

Structural barriers

There will be conflict when young people perceive or have evidence of unfair treatment. This could be when a young person perceives that someone else obtains an additional ten minutes using a computer game in comparison to his or her usage. The youth worker's response to structural barriers might be to create systems within youth clubs ensuring young people get fair and equal use of resources.

Table 7.2, adapted from Wheal (2006: 79), illustrates the gap between young people's behaviour and the underlying issues or cause. For example, the underlying issue rationalizing a young person's refusal

Table 7.2 Young person's behaviour and underlying issues

Young person's behaviour	Underlying issue
Refuses to do something	Can't do something
Says it's stupid	Doesn't understand
Won't speak	Doesn't know what to say
Rants and raves	Is embarrassed
Acts the fool	Is unsure
Gets angry	Needs attention
Shows off	Is worried

to participate in an activity could be caused by embarrassment or a lack of understanding of the activity, or could indicate that they are seeking additional attention from the youth worker.

Be proactive

One of my favourite artists is Banksy. One of his images shows a maid sweeping dust under the carpet – a perfect image of how I used to respond when faced with a difficult situation or conflict. At the time I was working as a mentor in a secondary school where I used Steve Covey's (2004) principles to frame conversations with young people. I found the principle 'be proactive', which values initiative, opposing indifference and taking responsibility for my actions, challenging. Back then, when I faced conflict or a difficult situation with a young person or a colleague where my natural inclination was to avoid any confrontation, I would say to myself, 'I must respond.' This act of being proactive was key to my development as a youth worker, because over time this kind of response became an automatic element of my practice. For example, ignoring a young person's lateness to a small group activity is a strategy, but doing nothing is not.

Wheal (2006: 75–8) gives a number of strategies for dealing with conflict that are relevant to managing all forms of challenging behaviour in a small group setting, as illustrated in Table 7.3.

Roles

Brierley (2003: 93–6) proposed eight roles young people play in a group setting. Table 7.4 illustrates a summary of the key points.

Table 7.3 Strategies for managing behaviour

Non-verbal signal	Eye contact, frown, glare
Close proximity	Simply moving closer to the young person
Redirection/praise	'That looks interesting, well done, shall we try . . . ?'
Active listening	Reflecting back the young person's feelings
Humour	Not sarcasm
Relocating	Suggest the young person moves to another seat or area
Ignoring	Sometimes the best strategy; however, ensure the situation doesn't escalate

Table 7.4 Roles young people play in groups

Group role	Brief description	Benefit to group	Challenge to youth worker
Dominator	Stands out, centre of attention	Draws a crowd	Always right
Spectator	Shy, opposite of dominator	Never misses a week	Difficult to figure out
Gladiator	Fight or flight type	Loyal, especially to vulnerable members	Reducing incidences of flight
Placator	Peacekeeper	Unites group members	Inability to handle conflict
Motivator	Motivates the group	Motivates	Intimidating
Terminator	Ensures ideas from group are practical and realistic	Identifies problems	Risk of negativity
Orator	Ditsy/opinionated personality	Gets discussion going	Distracts group
Actor	Joker	Fun	Prevents discussions from going deeper

'Dominators' (Brierley 2003: 93) can be popular and are key to the initial group set-up, as they will invite their friends. They are also frequently the centre of attention and can pose a challenge to even the most experienced facilitator. They can possess the need to ask a dozen questions or will contribute their opinion at every opportunity, leading you to suspect they like the sound of their own voice!

Therefore you need to strike a balance: being in control enough to facilitate the group's agenda (and not dominator's) but giving opportunity for the dominator to practise his or her leadership skills. I have merged Brierley's (2003: 96) 'actor' and 'orator' role as they often come together: this young person will make frequent jokes and contribute ditsy and irrelevant comments that will distract the group, most frustrating when conversation turns to serious or spiritual matters. Sadly, I've seen young people in this category become marginalized, mocked and the butt of jokes in a group from other young people and even volunteers. Being known as the idiot of the group is harmful because it damages their self-esteem and devalues their potential. The beauty of actor–orators is that they pull the group together in a way a youth worker is unable to and often just need the guidance of an adult to know when humorous comments are unhelpful.

The 'spectator' (Brierley 2003: 94) is quiet by nature and would give a limited response to a direct question. Brierley comments on causes for the spectator's behaviour, such as boredom, intense shyness or poor communication skills. I would add that the spectator has low confidence. In this case it is important that you or other young people do not do anything that might embarrass spectators (e.g. they are often softly spoken so are more susceptible to interruptions from others), causing them to withdraw even more in the future. Spectators might be drawn out of their shells by reassuring comments and body language over time. In addition, a spectator might be a reflector – a learning style where a young person needs time to think something through. Reflectors prefer to listen, and feel uncomfortable in unplanned situations or when asked their opinion on the spot.

Challenging behaviour is not a disease

Jesus' teaching centres strongly on treating others as we would like to be treated, through the second most important commandment: 'love your neighbour as yourself' (Matthew 22.39). Therefore we must avoid labelling the problematic parts of a young person's behaviour, focusing on the person and not the behaviour. Jesus is the ultimate example from which all youth workers can learn in responding to people, clearly seen when the adulterous woman was forgiven. Focusing solely on behaviour is dehumanizing and contrary to

Christ, who came to give humanity fullness of life (John 10.10). Young people are made in the image of God (Genesis 1.27), are valuable in the sight of God (Matthew 6.26) and worthy of God's demonstration of love (Romans 5.8).

Conclusion

Being a boundary marker is not always an easy task but it is rewarding as we see young people develop and flourish. The good news is that God will give us wisdom if we ask (James 1.5) in learning how to respond to challenging behaviour. However, it is key that our own journey with God is meaningful to ensure our attitudes and motives behind our words and actions on a daily basis are godly and reflect Christ (Philippians 1.27a, 4.8; Ephesians 4.29). If we are tired and feel distant from God, this may be reflected in our work with young people, shown in my attitude towards Griff that night. As we seek to work with young people, we must establish boundaries in creating a work–life balance and develop strategies for our own self-care (Matthew 11.28) – physical, emotional and spiritual.

Questions for reflection

- What are the positives and negatives of your facilitation style?
- What biblical perspectives come to mind when developing boundaries with young people?
- Write down dynamics among young people in your group that concern you. What action do you need to take to better manage the dynamics among young people in your group?
- A fight breaks out in your youth club. What immediate, short-term and long-term strategies would you put in place?

References and further reading

Bailey, K. E., 2008. *Jesus through Middle Eastern Eyes*. London, SPCK.

Brierley, D., 2003. *Growing Community: Making groups work with young people*. Cumbria, Authentic Lifestyle. Explores the process of engaging young people in small groups.

Cameron, E., 2005. *Facilitation Made Easy: Practical tips to improve meetings and workshops*. London, Kogan Page.

Cloud, H. and Townsend, J., 1992. *Boundaries: When to say yes, when to say no, to take control of your life*. Grand Rapids, MI, Zondervan. Offers helpful insights into how to set healthy boundaries in your personal and professional life.

Covey, S., 2001. *Seven Habits of Highly Effective People.* London, Simon and Schuster.

Dean, K. C., Clark, C. and Rahn, D. (eds), 2001. *Starting Right: Thinking theologically about youth ministry.* Grand Rapids, MI, Zondervan.

McGrath, A., 2007. *Christian Theology: An introduction,* fourth edition. Oxford, Blackwell.

Pimlott, J. and Pimlott, N., 2005. *Responding to Challenging Behaviour.* Cambridge, Grove Books. Concise and essential reading on responding to challenging behaviour.

Sapin, K., 2009. *Essential Skills for Youth Work Practice.* London, Sage.

Wheal, A., 2006. *Adolescence: Positive approaches to working with young people,* second edition. Lyme Regis: Russell House Publishing. Another practical book on understanding adolescents.

8

Mediating mirror

SAM RICHARDS

When I was a child, I talked like a child, I thought like a child, I rea-
soned like a child. When I became a man, I put childish ways behind
me. Now we see but a poor reflection as in a mirror; then we shall
see face to face. Now I know in part; then I shall know fully, even as
I am fully known.   (1 Corinthians 13.11–12, NIV)

Introduction – reflections in 'mirrors'

Young people are in the transition period between the two stages that
St Paul is talking about: childhood and adulthood. If, as adults, we
only have a poor or partial reflection of ourselves, a less than perfect
sense of who we are and what we are like; then young people may
have a very shaky, out-of-focus self-image.

We all unconsciously check our reflection as we walk past a mirror
or shop window. In fact some of us will hold our tummies in while we
look, to improve the image we see! Similarly, we all unconsciously
check how we are reflected in the eyes of other people, how we think
they see us. We look for approval, for signs that we are liked, that
others want to spend time with us. We are sensitive to any indications

to the contrary. Young people are incredibly concerned with how they think they are seen by others. Romances are pursued and fights are started on the basis of how someone thought someone else looked at them!

We are also sensitive to images in the media that we think relate to us. We compare ourselves to these images, and are aware that other people measure us against these images too. Young people are bombarded with images in the most image-saturated society to date. Many media images of young people are negative. They focus on the minority who are seen as trouble-makers, undertaking activities which are labelled anti-social, threatening and illegal. Young people know that these images do not accurately reflect their lives but nonetheless influence how others see them. In my own village I conducted a youth consultation as part of the research conducted to enable children and young people to contribute to the construction of a Village Plan. Over 50 per cent commented on adult attitudes to young people, and one thing the teenagers thought would improve village life would be 'for adults to be non-judgemental towards young people', 'they could talk to us rather than cross roads to avoid us', 'talk to us and see we're not so threatening'. (All quotes are taken from young people contributing to the Chalgrove Youth Consultation 2008.)

In this sense, we are constantly looking for mirrors to give us some feedback on how we are viewed and therefore some sense of who we are. Other people are at best faulty or cloudy mirrors, and at worst deliberately distorting mirrors like those found at funfairs. Christians believe that God is the one true mirror who can enable us to see ourselves as we really are, because that is how he sees us. For we are truly naked before our maker (Genesis 2.25), and not in order to look good! God's gaze is one of love. He is 'the LORD, the LORD, the compassionate and gracious God, slow to anger, abounding in love and faithfulness, maintaining love to thousands, and forgiving wickedness, rebellion and sin' (Exodus 34.6–7, NIV). He has made us in his image (Genesis 1.27) and longs for us to reflect fully the life of Jesus Christ, to reach our full potential as his children (John 1.12). Christian youth workers, therefore, have the opportunity to be mediating mirrors for the young people they work among. We can seek to reflect back to young people both how we see them and how God sees them, and help them to reject unhelpful self-images they have received from elsewhere.

Identity

Identity is the mind's eye picture we have of ourselves. One of the things that distinguishes us as human beings is our ability to internally reflect and consider who we are. It is important to have as sharp an image of ourselves as possible. We may not like all we see, but seeing an image in focus helps us at least to know what is there. This helps us in two ways: first, to know that we are special and unique, which is vital for good self-esteem and a foundation of the Christian faith. We all need to know that we matter and are worth something. We are all of immense value to God, being made in his image and so loved by him that in the greatest act of love he gave his life for us.

Second, it helps us to know what to expect from ourselves, which is a huge asset in a complex and uncertain world. It is one less thing to worry about, particularly in social settings. We are then free to concentrate on other people's reactions and external circumstances. We are able to rely on who we are, and our responses, and have a sense of being a coherent and consistent person. A clear sense of identity enables us to make decisions and act boldly.

Self-esteem

Self-esteem is in essence a measure of how much we like ourselves. Common sense and everyday dealings with people tell us that low self-esteem is not good for people and greatly reduces their ability to enjoy life and relate well to other people; while high self-esteem gives people self-confidence and self-assurance, enabling them to take risks, receive criticism, be more open with others and be less easily swayed by outside pressure. Jesus said, 'I have come that they may have life, and have it to the full' (John 10.10, NIV). Enabling others to develop a good self-image and positive self-esteem may be seen as part of the good news of Jesus Christ.

Building blocks of self-esteem

1 *A sense of moral worth* Everyone needs to feel they are basically an OK person, that they are one of the 'good guys'. Young people are in the process of working out what counts as good and right in ethical choices. They may be rejecting the rules and values of

authority as they try to find their own, and so be on the receiving end of someone else's definition of them as immoral (for example, school, parents, church).

2 *A sense of competence* Everyone needs to know they are good at something, successful in some field. Our sense of competence is our level of ability divided by our level of expectation, so our self-esteem will increase if our achievements increase or if our aims decrease. For example, if I hope to swim 50 lengths but only manage 30 my self-esteem sinks; however, if I hope to swim 25 and achieve 30, I feel positively buoyant! Teenagers are being formally assessed at school against impersonal standards and may feel the weight of parental expectation. They often seek other arenas (such as fashion, skate-boarding, drinking, mis-behaving) where they can gain a sense of competence from their peers.

3 *A sense of self-determination* Everyone needs to feel they have some control over their lives. People who feel their lives are ruled entirely by fate, or others around them, have a low image of themselves and consequently have no energy to stand up for themselves. Young people often feel they are being asked to make decisions they feel ill equipped for (such as career choice or which parent to live with following a break-up), while not being given freedom to make the choices they want to about their lives (how late to stay out, who to hang out with).

4 *A sense of unity* Everyone needs to know that their feelings, beliefs and actions add up to one whole person, rather than parts of a variety of people. Teenagers often examine the roles they play and the different ways they behave in different settings and especially around different groups of people, and feel that they are one person at home and quite another with their friends. They feel something of a chameleon. Hormonal changes due to puberty can also mean they find their own emotional reactions unpredictable and changeable.

All four of these building blocks for self-esteem can be problematic for any young person, however smooth or bumpy that individual's journey through adolescence may be. It is important for us to consider how we can respond to these, and through our youth ministry offer opportunities to develop in such areas.

Identity development in adolescence

Most theorists (e.g. Blos, Erikson, Kegan, Kohlberg and Loevinger – see Kroger 2004) agree that adolescence is an important period in the development of our identity. It is a key time in constructing a framework robust enough and yet flexible enough to see us through the rest of our lives, with their many stresses and crises. It also needs to be solid enough for us to risk venturing into intimate relationships, when we allow others to get to know who we really are; or to express our identity in creative effort and show our real 'self' to the outside world. It is in our teens that we begin to have an inner sense of who we are. This is one reason why youth work is so exciting. Young people we work among are in the very process of forming the basis of their adult identity, and so are looking for ideas, opinions, experiences, theories and people worth basing their very selves upon. Erikson (1994) proposes that successfully negotiating the construction of identity in adolescence enables people to develop the virtue of **fidelity**: the ability to be faithful to a person or belief. Bearing in mind that identity and fidelity are both in the process of development during adolescence, I developed some guidelines for good practice as a Christian youth worker. Rather than a traditional 'altar call', I would invite young people to commit as much of themselves as they could to as much as they knew of Jesus. Such a moment of commitment remained a significant landmark on a journey of faith, but one that could be revisited and reaffirmed as their sense of themselves changed, and their knowledge of Jesus grew.

Labels that stick

> George Herbert Mead (1934) said that humans are 'talked into' our humanity. He meant that we gain personal identity as we communicate with others. In the earliest years of our lives, our parents tell us who we are: 'You're smart.' 'You're so strong.' 'You're such a clown.' We first see ourselves through the eyes of others, so their messages form important foundations of our self-concepts. Later, we interact with teachers, friends, romantic partners, and co-workers who communicate their views to us. Thus, how we see ourselves reflects the views of us that others communicate.
> (Wood 2009: 5)

This means that it is important to be careful what we say to young people. The same behaviour can be labelled and defined in either positive or negative ways, thereby attributing meaning and values: for example, flexible or wishy-washy, firm or stubborn, courageous or foolhardy, sensible or chicken, generous or wasteful, thrifty or tight-fisted, enthusiastic or unstable, steady or dull (Griffin 1987). As youth workers, we need to be able to appreciate the wide diversity of attributes God has given to his people in their multi-characterful, multi-cultural and multi-gifted variety. Remember that we are created to be a part of a body made up of many different parts, all with their own strengths to contribute to the whole: 'If the whole body were an eye, where would the hearing be?' (1 Corinthians 12.17).

As youth workers we can look for opportunities to do such positive labelling. This is so important because often the only behaviour that elicits comment from adults is negative behaviour – being told off or disciplined. We can seek to provide a positive commentary on young people's actions, as a sports commentator would on a match, during youth work activities. This can feel rather strange at first, but it is a good way to ensure that we are naming and responding to all the behaviour we appreciate (such as persevering, encouraging others, asking questions, sharing, taking turns, contributing appropriately, team work, patience, listening, etc.). We can give a commentary on any activity, from a game to a discussion, and ensure we positively label everyone's behaviour in some way. Another opportunity we have for this positive labelling is in one-to-one work. Here we can provide some feedback on an individual's development in areas of character and behaviour, enabling him or her to see and celebrate every small step forward as positive.

Strokes

Eric Berne developed an approach to understanding human interactions called 'transactional analysis' (see Berne 1964). He believed that everyone needs to be recognized by others, and called any word, greeting, gesture or touch that recognized another's presence a **stroke**. Berne defined a stroke as the 'fundamental unit of social action' (1964: 15). Research has shown that small children need physical contact to thrive, and that as they grow older they learn to substitute words and gestures for physical strokes. So while an infant needs cuddling, an adult craves a smile, a wink, a hand gesture or other form of recognition. Berne called this requirement of adults to receive strokes

recognition-hunger. Berne argued that such strokes can be **positive** (complimentary, affectionate, leaving the other person feeling alive and significant) or **negative** (put-down, insult) but that either is better than no stroke at all (being ignored and given no recognition). Positive strokes are sometimes called 'Warm Fuzzies' and negative strokes 'Cold Prickles' (see Freed 1973) as this describes how they can make us feel when we receive them.

The best stroke is a positive unconditional stroke that communicates 'I like you – you're OK', with no strings attached. It must be genuine and honest. A **super-stroke** is one that comes from a very special person about something that is very important to you. As a young person's mentor or discipler we may hold this position and be able to give a super-stroke about that person's progress towards a personal goal or development and expression of a particular character attribute. We need to practise being specific, concrete and genuine in these comments to young people, so that they are able to receive them and give them full value. What a privilege to be able to do this – 'love builds up' (1 Corinthians 8.1).

Some people who have difficulty accumulating enough positive strokes may become skilful at acquiring negative strokes. You may work with some young people like this, who seem to make it very difficult to give them any positive strokes. They become accustomed to negative strokes and so seem to dismiss or shrug off any positive strokes you offer them; these do not make sense to them and so are not received. However, they seem to pull negative strokes out of you, almost despite yourself! This is because negative strokes reinforce what they already think they know about themselves so they make sense to them. We may have to work extra hard to enable such a young person to receive a positive stroke – here non-verbal strokes (gestures, smiles, showing we are listening) may be more successful at first.

Body image

Young people experience dramatic changes to their bodies as they leave their child bodies behind and develop adult bodies capable of reproducing. They are becoming sexual beings, experiencing sexual attraction and fretting about their own attractiveness to others. Body image is a huge issue for many young people who feel that their body is not 'normal', is ugly and fails to meet up to the standards pro-moted in the media. Some take refuge in eating disorders, self-harm or over-sexualized behaviour to avoid their disappointment or disgust with their own body. As Christians, in our work among young people we need to challenge this obsession with image. 'People look at the outward appearance, but the LORD looks at the heart' (1 Samuel 16.7, TNIV). We need to find creative ways to put external appearance in the bigger context of identity and character.

Two colleagues at Oxford Youth Works ran an innovative pro-gramme for girls with very low body image and confidence. They watched carefully chosen movies together and discussed how women were portrayed. They then organized a photo-shoot that involved the girls doing each other's hair and make-up, dressing each other up and then helping each other pose. The results were an enormous boost to their self-esteem: for the first time they saw themselves as beautiful. This was reinforced by comments on the photographs from families and friends. However, this sense of beauty was not just external and temporary, but more importantly internal and lasting, as they had treated each other as truly beautiful people. The photos now act as permanent reminders of this both publicly (posted on Facebook) and privately (displayed at home).

Looking-glass self

> O wad some Power the giftie gie us
> To see oursels as ithers see us!

> O would some Power the gift to give us
> To see ourselves as others see us!
> (from Robert Burns, 'To a Louse', 1786)

Cooley (1922) developed the idea of the **looking-glass self**. He argued that this affects us all without our realizing, but sometimes we only become aware of it when we experience a significant change in our lives. Cooley described a three-stage unconscious process of how we construct this looking-glass self. First, we imagine how we appear to others. Second, we imagine the reaction of others to our (imagined) appearance. Then, third, we evaluate ourselves according to how we imagine others have judged us, either positively or negatively. Because the looking-glass comes from our imagination, it can be distorted and not accurately reflect other people's opinion of us. Unfortunately, regardless of whether or not we are correct or incorrect about their perception, the consequences to how we feel about ourselves are just as real: 'I don't think they liked me; therefore they don't like me.'

This looking-glass self process can also apply to our relationship with God – we respond emotionally to how we imagine God thinks about us, and that in turn impacts our relationship with God. It is vital that we are able to offer young people opportunities to reflect on who they are and to start to have glimpses of their identity in Christ. We need to enable young people to find and develop a faith that connects meaningfully to their identity and that builds their self-esteem. Such a faith should show them that they are of immense value and can develop moral worth. Such a faith gives them the confidence to respond to the call of God on their life, to develop skills and competence as they pursue their vocation. Such a faith takes seriously their ability to choose and to change with the Spirit's help, to determine their own response to God. Such a faith integrates who they are and holds them together individually and as part of a larger body.

Questions for reflection

- Finish the sentence 'I am . . .' in 15 different ways to create a list of statements that sum up what you consider most important about who you are. Spend some time reflecting on this list with a good friend or prayer partner, looking at the roles, relationships and characteristics you have identified. What does your friend think you have left out?
- Reflect on examples from the Gospel of Luke when Jesus addresses these areas of different people's lives. How could these inspire your ministry among young people?
  - A sense of moral worth – Zacchaeus (Luke 19.1–10)
  - A sense of competence – sending out the 72 disciples (Luke 10.1–24)
  - A sense of self-determination – healing blind beggar (Luke 18.35–42)
  - A sense of unity – healing the demon-possessed man (Luke 8.26–39).
- Think of a phrase or word often used to describe you as a child (usually by parents or significant adults) which may be part of 'family folklore' now. What did this feel like at the time? What

does it feel like now? Are there any negative consequences for how you think about yourself or behave now? Are there any positive consequences for how you think about yourself or behave now?

- Reflect over the last 24 hours. How many positive strokes can you remember receiving? How many can you remember giving? Practise identifying specific behaviours and character attributes that you can comment on positively and concretely within your youth work – try to give some super-strokes tomorrow.
- Do you dress or get ready for yourself or for how others see you? Who are your most important significant others? How is this quote an example of looking-glass self? 'No one can make you feel inferior without your consent' (Eleanor Roosevelt).

References and further reading

Berne, E., 1964. *Games People Play*. New York, Grove Press.

Cooley, C., 1922. *Human Nature and the Social Order*. New York, Scribner's.

Erikson, E., 1994. *Identity: Youth and Crisis*. New York, W. W. Norton.

Etherton, L., 2008. *Self-esteem and Young People*. Cambridge, Grove. Practical and accessible booklet.

Freed, A., 1973. *TA for Tots and Other Prinzes*. Sacramento, Jalmar Press. Fun introduction to transactional analysis.

Griffin, E., 1987. *Making Friends and Making Them Count*. Downers Grove, IVP.

Kroger, J., 2004. *Identity in Adolescence*, third edition. Hove, Routledge. Comprehensive overview.

Mead, G., 1936. *Mind, Self, and Society*. Chicago, University of Chicago Press.

Wood, J., 2009. *Communication in Our Lives*. Boston: Wadsworth/Cengage Learning.

9

Guardian of souls

JO WHITEHEAD WITH SARA REYNOLDS

> The art of living soulfully is different for everyone. There is no one
> soul size; they come in all shapes and sizes. What makes one soul sing
> may singe another. (Leonard Sweet)

The idea of being a 'guardian of souls' may conjure up some powerful images in our minds – guardian angels, perhaps, or quests in *Lord
of the Rings*-type films, where something precious is contested or
sought. The phrase also has resonances of the traditional role of
parish priests as those with spiritual responsibility for their 'flock'.
'This is the pastoral work that is historically termed the cure of
souls . . . the Scripture-directed, prayer-shaped care that is devoted
to persons singly or in groups, in settings sacred and profane' (Peterson
1989: 57). This definition helps us grasp something of what it means
to be a guardian of souls. The word 'guardian' means 'defender',
'protector' or 'keeper' or 'a person legally responsible for someone
unable to manage their own affairs' (*Concise Oxford Dictionary*).
The concept thus carries a sense of protection, defence, keeping,
nurturing, but without undermining the autonomy of those being
cared for. Indeed, in youth ministry, guardians of souls should
rather encourage individuals to take responsibility themselves, and

88

provide safe space, support and encouragement as young people seek to develop their spirituality and faith.

Spiritual and faith development

> Spiritual development is not something we can do for others. It is a journey that each individual has to take. The journey cannot be made easier by taking short cuts and everyone has their own starting point and final destination. (Pimlott *et al.* 2005: 13)

While spiritual development models can be helpful to us, it is important to recognize that no aspect of development takes place in isolation. A young person's spiritual development is intrinsically linked to and affected by other areas of growth.

Concepts of spiritual and faith development have been subject to much debate and discussion. Maxine Green (2006) highlights the challenge of defining the term 'spirituality', when it is attractive to some and laden with baggage for others. Although people belonging to a particular faith group may use 'spirituality' and 'spiritual development' in relation to their faith, these terms also include broader aspects, such as 'awareness that there is more to life than meets the eye, an understanding that life is full of things that inspire awe and wonder, a rationale that incorporates paradoxes, the unexplained and mysteries' (Pimlott *et al.* 2005: 11). Most youth ministers engage young people in faith development and will also perhaps be seeking to support those who do not yet have a personal faith to explore and develop their spirituality.

James Fowler uses 'faith development' to describe the place that finding meaning and value have in identity development 'against a background of shared meaning and purpose' (1995: 4). He identifies seven stages to faith development (National Society 1991), with a progression from foundation faith in infancy to a 'selfless' faith in the final stage. He defines the third stage, 'conforming' faith, as being typical of 11- to 18-year-olds, identifying individuals in this stage as being conscious of the values that shape them and give them meaning (Fowler 1995: 152). They are also deeply influenced by 'chosen authority figures' (National Society 1991: 25) who can be friends, family members, teachers, youth ministers or church leaders. Fowler proposes that the developing acknowledgement of the need for integration, or drawing things together, causes adolescents to seek not only meaning but also someone who 'knows, accepts and confirms the self deeply' (1995: 153). At this stage young people are not yet reflecting critically on their own values but are aware of holding strong values and norms, which they invest in, are emotionally attached to and will defend strongly (Fowler 1995). In our youth group, the young people got really engaged in issues around fair-trading and inequality and oppression in both this and other countries. Particular individuals were influenced by their involvement and the increasing coherence of their values was evident in the active role they took in promoting these issues both within the group and with friends. (Sara collated the stories in this chapter, and they represent the work of youth workers from a variety of traditions and contexts.)

In Fowler's theory, 'conforming' faith is followed for some by 'choosing' faith, where individuals begin to create meaning for themselves, rather than drawing it from those around them. This aspect of growth can be confusing and disorientating for some, who may experience questioning, doubt and a sense of loss before they discover a new, more mature faith. Westerhoff (1976) has a similar understanding of adolescent faith development, seeing younger adolescents in a stage of 'affiliative faith' where belonging and the influence of significant others are key to the journey. In later adolescence, he proposes, they move into 'searching faith', questioning previously held beliefs and experimenting with other understandings and ideologies.

Relationship – being there

The young people taught me about youth work and the long haul – that discipleship isn't about what material you use or what you teach but who you are, and there's something in that they see. It's like I don't know how or what I do but it happens. It's about relationship, not material, and not judging them when they open their lives to you. To be an effective guardian of souls we must, first and foremost, be present, with and for young people. It is in and through relationships that we earn the right and find effective ways to support young people in the development of their faith and spirituality. Our presence is significant both in the need for belonging which characterizes the early teenage years, and in the potential questioning and searching which follow later in adolescence. We took a group of young people to Soul Survivor and one of the young people responded to the opportunity to make a commitment to God. When she responded it was like she had thought about it already and that was just the opportunity to do so, I don't think it was a sudden awareness of what God meant to her, but came out of five years of discipleship.

Jesus himself models working with a small group of dedicated followers in a three-year, life-sharing and ultimately life-transforming experience. In this 'sharing of life', Jesus lived and walked and taught and ate and laughed and cried with those he worked with. So often we can underestimate the importance of 'ordinary' time spent with young people and the ways in which we are able to nurture them in everyday contexts. Young people spend only a fraction of their lives in a church or youth group. The vast majority of time is spent with friends, family, in school, college or work, undertaking hobbies or interests, relaxing, consuming media, etc. The dualism by which many Christian young people live is increasingly recognized (Pimlott and Pimlott 2008), as they portray their identity differently in different contexts. We need to equip them to live out their faith in their whole world. Seeing how we respond to everyday pressures and making connections between life and faith are essential if young people are to understand what faith looks like in all the places they spend their lives.

> It is not a narrowing of pastoral work to its devotional aspects but it is a way of life that uses weekday tasks, encounters, and situations as the raw material for teaching prayer, developing faith, and preparing for a good death.
> (Peterson 1989: 59)

A significant aspect of 'being with' young people is the intentional nature of our relationships with them. In exploring the ministry of spiritual direction, Margaret Guenther uses the metaphor of hospitality – 'a gift of space, both physical and spiritual' (1993: 13). Within the spaces we create with young people, it is important to be intentional. It should be completely natural for us to talk about faith, yet many in youth ministry find this difficult. Our experience suggests young people – both within and outside church – are very open to talking about personal faith and spirituality and we need to be explicit in our conversations (Collins-Mayo *et al.* 2010).

Community – being together

'A young person's faith is best tended by a variety of relationships within a Christian community' (Yaconelli 2006: 101). Our consideration of faith development has highlighted the importance of a sense of belonging for young people in the 'conforming' (Fowler) or 'affiliative' (Westerhoff) stage. The experience of being part of something – a church, youth group, Bible study group, team, band – plays a significant part in many young people's developing understanding and experience of God. Although the ideal place for this would often be perceived to be a large, vibrant youth group, this often isn't possible and we need to think creatively about how to engender a sense of belonging, perhaps through smaller cell groups, prayer triplets or a buddying system. In one church young people are supported not only through groups but as individuals; each young person is given a 'buddy' from within the church who can mentor and be there for them. Strong friendships have developed through the groups themselves and the individual discipling that happens.

Challenging church cultures where work with young people is seen as the preserve of a select few can be difficult, but is crucial. We have seen instances where young people have deliberately chosen to attend smaller churches with less apparently youth-friendly approaches, simply because adults in the congregation spoke to them and welcomed them. Many adults who are not involved in youth programmes may be willing to spend time one-to-one with a young person.

Understanding the importance of community and belonging will help us consider the extent to which activities are designed to develop and deepen relationships. Many young people go to groups to see friends rather than to learn about God, yet we can see social and relational aspects as separate from the 'proper' God stuff. Recognizing the spiritual importance of friendships in faith development will help us give them priority in our planning. We can ensure we create space for relationships to develop, giving time for informal conversation, social activities and creative interaction. A programme-driven approach can push out some of these key relational opportunities. Some of our deepest 'God conversations' with young people have been unplanned and unexpected rather than part of a set programme.

Within structured youth work, having 'safe' space where young people feel they can be real and openly share faith, struggles, joys and doubts is of paramount importance. One group reports:

> We have seen young people owning their faith for themselves, moving from a corporate faith, existing first within the group, to a personal faith, existing first in their own lives. As a group we have grown to a place where we can be honest about our lives and our struggles. We have become a community that supports and cares for one another, but also challenges each other when we don't live up to what we say we want. This is something we now build into our youth work programme, so that we don't take for granted that we are automatically moving to where we want to be.

Encountering – being with God

> We don't need to 'deliver' God to young people. We simply need to help young people notice the ways in which each and every one of them is already in relationship with God. Our role is to help young people notice the ways in which Jesus is already near, already seeking trust and friendship.
>
> (Yaconelli 2006: 136)

If we are to support young people in developing their own relationship with God, one of the most significant things we can do is to provide opportunities for them to encounter God for themselves. This may sound obvious, but in a church culture characterized by busyness and activity, and a broader culture where young people are almost constantly stimulated by noise, images and technology, it is quite a challenge. For some, this will most effectively be accomplished in formal worship contexts; for others it will involve carving out sacred space in other ways. As one youth worker writes:

> I work in both a Pentecostal and URC church and although they are very different both have been effective at discipling and the young people talk about enjoying being there. In both the important thing has been about creating space to reflect on their learning and experiences. Prayer has been important in helping the young people to see an integration in their lives; they can bring everything that is important to them to it.

Many are finding the use of contemplative and traditional approaches to prayer and worship helpful in helping young people intentionally connect with God (Baker and Ratnayake 2004; Yaconelli 2006).

We need to be confidently explicit about faith, tell the story and avoid assuming young people are familiar with what the Christian faith means or what it implies in terms of lifestyle. We also need to be aware of the church culture we are in and the culture we are creating ourselves. We are likely to have expectations on the young people who are part of our groups – some of which will be articulated, others hidden. Young people who begin to question and doubt may feel they no longer 'fit' because of their exploring, and may drift away if we haven't created relational environments where they feel they can be real and honest without feeling judged or condemned. A youth worker tells how some young people wanted to go a bit deeper in their faith:

> They wanted to look at questions 'where the answer wasn't always Jesus'. I was aiming for it to be a safe place where they could say what they thought or felt. At first they found this really challenging as I was constantly saying there wasn't a right or wrong answer, but that two people in the group could think differently from each other and from me. After a while it needed a bit of mixing up. Some wanted to look at questions they were often challenged about at school, so we looked at creation and evolution, sex before marriage, etc. There wasn't much material on this and it needed some thoughtful reading, which on a Thursday evening was often too much to expect for some.

We should be seeking to encourage young people to develop their own relationship with God within their own personality, interests and cultures rather than to produce clones of ourselves, and encouraging dependence on God more than dependence on ourselves. There is a tension here. We need to be dependable, and for some (particularly younger) young people we may need to 'be Jesus' for a while, but our ultimate aim will be to seek to assist young people, as they transition through adolescence, to become autonomous and take responsibility for their own faith journey.

Power and participation – being involved

When it comes to the area of spiritual growth and discipleship we need to be particularly aware of the 'weight' of our role and the power it brings. We may not *feel* particularly powerful, but in many young people's eyes we are likely to be seen as those with authority, because of our title, our role, our age, our personality and other factors. Although the term 'spiritual abuse' can sound extreme, the effects of abuse of power, when it has a spiritual dimension, can become multi-plied. Abuse of power in youth ministry contexts can manifest itself in unhealthy dependence of young people on a youth leader, author-itarian leadership styles, manipulation, control, heavy shepherding, excessive discipline and/or spiritual intimidation (Beasley-Murray 1998). In our experience most misuse of power in church contexts is not a deliberate attempt to inflict harm, but rather emerges out of insecurity, fear, a desire for control and/or to see people 'do the right thing'. Nevertheless, benevolent oppression is still oppression, and self-awareness in this area is vital.

As we have already identified, our role as guardians of souls is not to do the spiritual growth for young people, but rather to support them in growing and becoming autonomous, making their own decisions and discovering God for themselves. There is a tension here in many church cultures where there can be a pressure on youth workers to encourage young people to conform. However, experience would suggest that young people simply doing what the youth worker wants can lead to dualism: they say what they think we want to hear and then go and do what they want anyway. It is interesting to consider that Jesus gave people choices and sometimes let them walk away (Luke 19.22). We often face a dilemma in relation to large-scale events. After taking our discipleship group to big worship events, seeing them respond and then come home to church and lose the passion they had while away, our youth team decided that we needed to speak to them about what they really wanted. Until this point it had been taken for granted that the young people wanted to grow in God, but it was never actually discussed. So we opened up the conversation and asked them what they wanted for their faith, where they wanted to go with God and what we could do to support them in that. We are quite a close-knit group, and have built a foundation of trust with the group, so the young people knew they could be brutally honest with us. This turned out to be a very positive step and gave the young people the opportunity to reflect on their faith, and their responsibility in growing it.

Learning and growing – being a disciple

We are all fundamentally called to be disciples of Christ. As those who seek to input into others we must be committed to ongoing learning and growth ourselves, modelling something in and through our own relationship with God, our willingness to learn from others, openness to being challenged and accountability. This requires being real and disclosing something of our own spiritual journey, without being inappropriate or dominating relationships with our own agendas. Sharing our life in God will mean praying both with and for the young people and engaging in other spiritual disciplines with them, where appropriate.

An acknowledgement of struggle will assist young people in growing a faith that is owned, robust and resilient. The dangers of a hothouse-style, over-protective faith context, where questioning is discouraged and the Christian is always victorious, happy and certain, is that young people don't develop the capacity to wrestle with issues, face questions and engage in theological reflection. Acknowledging questioning and doubt as normal and positive will help provide safe space for resilience to develop. This kind of resilience is like a tree, which is flexible and supple enough to bend in strong winds, but whose roots go deep, enabling it to stand strong in storms.

Above all, as a guardian of souls, our role is recognizing and acknowledging what God is doing in young people's lives and seeking to support and work alongside him. As we trust the Holy Spirit in young people's lives, we can care, support, encourage, challenge and nurture young people as they continue their faith journey or develop their spirituality.

Questions for reflection

- How do you understand the balance between supporting young people in their spiritual and faith development and seeing them take responsibility for this themselves?
- What approaches have you found helpful in assisting young people to grow spiritually?
- How could you develop your practice of 'hospitality' in the broadest sense of creating safe space for young people?
- In what ways are you investing in your own development as a disciple of Christ?

References and further reading

Baker, J. and Ratnayake, M., 2004. *Tune In, Chill Out*. Birmingham, Christian Education. Contemplative prayer resources to use with young people.

Beasley-Murray, P., 1998. *Power for God's Sake*. Carlisle, Paternoster.

Collins-Mayo, S., Mayo, B., Nash, S. and Cocksworth, C., 2010. *The Faith of Generation Y*. London, Church House Publishing. Comprehensive overview of issues around the spirituality and faith of young people today.

Fowler, J., 1995. *Stages of Faith: The psychology of human development and the quest for meaning*. New York, HarperCollins.

Green, M., 2006. *A Journey of Discovery: Spirituality and spiritual development in youth work*. Leicester, National Youth Agency.

Green, M. and Christian, C., 1998. *Accompanying Young People on their Spiritual Quest*. London, National Society and Church House Publishing. Good resource for considering empowering, non-directional ways of working with young people to encourage their spiritual development.

Guenther, M., 1993. *Holy Listening: The art of spiritual direction*. London, Darton, Longman and Todd.

National Society, 1991. *How Faith Grows: Faith development and Christian education*. London, National Society and Church House Publishing.

Peterson, E. H., 1989. *The Contemplative Pastor: Returning to the art of spiritual direction*. Grand Rapids, MI, Eerdmans.

Pimlott, J. and Pimlott, N., 2008. *Youth Work after Christendom*. Bletchley, Paternoster.

Pimlott, J., Pimlott, N. and Wiles, D., 2005. *Inspire Too! More fresh ideas for creative youth work*. Birmingham, FYT. Introductory ideas around spirituality, learning and journeying with young people, with resources CD.

Sweet, L., 2000. *Soul Salsa: Surprising steps for godly living in the 21st century*. Grand Rapids, MI, Zondervan.

Westerhoff, J., 1976. *Will Our Children Have Faith?*. New York, Seabury.

Yaconelli, M., 2006. *Contemplative Youth Ministry: Practising the presence of Jesus with young people*. London, SPCK. Exploring Jesus-centred ways of being with young people.

10

Odyssey guide

SALLY NASH AND BEV PALMER

I've learned that people will forget what you said, people will forget what you did, but people will never forget how you made them feel.

(Maya Angelou)

A cardinal point that we must keep constantly in mind, the lodestar which keeps us in course, as we negotiate the uncharted twists and turns of the struggle for liberation is that the breakthrough is never the results of individual effort. It is always a collective effort and triumph. (Nelson Mandela)

Adam was only 12, but he hung around with 16-year-olds. He engaged regularly in anti-social behaviour and was at risk of getting an ASBO (Anti Social Behaviour Order). Trying to get Adam to see that the group were using him as a puppet, pulling his strings whenever they needed a cheap laugh, did not work. He was attached, he felt accepted by them and they offered him the sense of community that his family, school and local community did not. Adam needed 'enlightened witnesses' to come alongside him and offer him a less distorted view of life and himself: someone who, while showing unconditional positive regard, would not excuse his behaviour but find reasons for it, and in so doing would offer him a different frame of reference. Asking him questions rather than delivering facts, being curious about him without being intrusive, coming alongside him without an agenda in part showed him that someone cared about his view of the world while not necessarily agreeing with it. The role of the youth worker in supporting Adam is like being a lighthouse, shining a beacon into the dark, alerting him to the dangers and hoping he will steer a different course. This is what we mean by being an odyssey guide. We may also liken it to the role of the Holy Spirit in our lives, being a comforter and guide, helping us on our journey.

Odyssey: a long and eventful or adventurous journey or process – just like adolescence! The word comes from Greek author Homer's epic poem (written about 8 BCE) telling the story of Odysseus' eventful journey home after victory at Troy (see <www.mythweb/odyssey/Odyssey.pdf>). As youth workers, one of the things we can offer young people is to be a guide on their journey towards adulthood, accompanying them in their wanderings, explorations, discoveries, decisions, dreams, failures and achievements. Naomi wanted a perspective on whether she was ready for the next step in Christian service she was contemplating – the youth worker confirmed that she was. Part of our role may be to identify areas for young people's development which are not so far beyond their capacity as to result in failure, but which develop and stretch them and perhaps help them overcome one of the challenges of their journey (Vygotsky's (1978) zone of proximal development). Another bit in the jigsaw for Naomi was to attend a vocations day. It will be fascinating to see how her journey unfolds. Other terms people may use for this sort of role are mentor, coach, discipler, accompanier, spiritual director.

Young people's journeys

Who we are at any point in time is about what we think, judge, feel, value, honour, esteem, hope, love, fear, desire, believe in and are committed to. These are the things that shape and define us as people and may change – particularly in adolescence. Erikson (1995) talks about two basic conflicts in adolescence: identity versus confusion in early adolescence and intimacy versus isolation in later adolescence. Part of a youth worker's role will be to try to mitigate against unfavourable outcomes of these conflicts. The hope is that young people emerge from these stages with a sense of achievement, knowing who they are and realizing they have the capacity to make and do things themselves.

The young people we accompany will all be at different stages on a spiritual journey and not necessarily Christian, but as Christian youth workers we want young people to find the life in all its fullness that Jesus talks about (John 10.10). We are offering young people our wisdom, as people a little further along in the journey, and God's wisdom which is 'something mysterious that goes deep into the interior of his purposes . . . what God determined as the way to bring out his best in us' (1 Corinthians 2.7, *The Message*). However, we must never forget that it is the young person's agenda we should be following, not our own. If we have any sense that we are trying to live our lives vicariously through the young people we work with then we need to address this – youth workers have power and it is vital that we use it to liberate, not oppress. It can be all too easy to hold back young people from following their dreams or making their own mistakes because we dismiss their naive utopian view of life.

Being an odyssey guide – qualities and tools

Many of us do youth work because, like Jeremiah (1.4–5), we have heard God's call, and because we love young people; to paraphrase Freire, 'It is impossible to be a youth worker without the courage to love' (2005: 5). Knowing that we are loved is such a vital experience and essential for a healthy adulthood. As youth workers we need to find ways of demonstrating this in appropriate and accessible ways in keeping with policies and good practice. Lefevre (2010: 34) summarizes what a young person needs to feel trusting and safe:

- kindness, supportiveness, a caring attitude and showing personal concern;
- empathy, sympathy, showing understanding;
- openness, genuineness, congruence and honesty;
- accepting and non-judgemental approach;
- respectful, friendly and warm in manner;
- accessibility and availability;
- consistency, trustworthiness and reliability.

When we read a list such as this it becomes clear that we don't need to know all the answers to work with young people. While some specialist skills are needed, what is vital is a desire and willingness to build a relationship and to be there for them, something we can encourage among others in the congregation too – an odyssey guide can take many forms.

Today it is so easy to be distracted by technology and to never be fully there for another as we wait for the next text or keep an eye on the progress of a match or Facebook discussion. We need to actively listen by paying full attention to the young person, making eye contact appropriately, accepting what he or she is saying, seeking to draw out the individual's thoughts and feelings and reflecting back to ensure we have understood what has been said. Feeling that we have been listened to can be a significant experience, and it is a particular privilege of being a youth worker that we get to listen to young people.

Jane presented as an intelligent articulate young woman. She was an accomplished musician and dancer and excelled at everything. What many of her peers did not know was that her perfectionism hid a self-belief that she was ugly to the core. She was a serious self-harmer, a young woman so broken and damaged on the inside that she did not really trust anyone, least of all herself. What happened to make her this way was only revealed over time – time that was given to just listening to her, accepting her and letting her know it was OK to be whoever she felt she needed to be at any given time. Showing her that all the fragments of herself were loveable and acceptable helped draw the pieces of herself back together. The relationship formed with the youth worker is still strong today, five years on. It is held together by the glue of safe boundaries of care and concern as well as availability and supportive challenge. The youth worker has remained a constant in an ever-changing inner and outer world, showing that healing can come in many ways. Some of us may think that we don't have the skills or experience to work with a young person like Jane, and in such a situation it is important both to refer to an agency or someone who does have the skills and to offer what we are able to, acceptance and presence. If we are moving on we also need to try and secure ongoing care for those we leave behind.

Empowerment is a core youth work value and an essential part of being an odyssey guide. This will involve being willing to let young people make mistakes, as often significant learning can come from our mistakes.

Jack really wasn't sure about going to university; he didn't see himself as being clever so decided not to apply and went off on his gap year. His youth worker realized that to push him when he wasn't sure it was the right thing for him would be counter-productive. As the year unfolded Jack found that to do what he really wanted he needed a degree and so, encouraged by his youth worker, he finally applied, graduated and got the job he wanted. If we have a tendency to want to rescue people, then it can be difficult to empower them to make their own decisions and mistakes and resist the temptation to say 'I told you so' when it all goes wrong. However, if we want young people to successfully become both autonomous and interdependent then they need to know that we respect and trust them yet are there for them when needed.

Vocation

Alice is walking about in Wonderland. Enchanted, she goes from one discovery to another. She comes upon a crossroads. She stops and wonders which path to take. She doesn't know what to do. Suddenly she notices a hare. She runs to meet him and says, 'I have come to a crossroads; could you tell me which path I should take?' The hare asks her 'Where do you want to go?' Shrugging her shoulders, Alice replies, 'I don't know!' 'Well then, young lady,' answers the hare, 'You may take either path.'   (Monbourquette 2003: 120)

Stories naturally are a good tool for an odyssey guide to use as they effectively communicate important truth in accessible ways. It took us a while to realize that there was no Plan A we must strive to find, and that God often gives us freedom to make choices as we seek to build the kingdom.

Part of being an odyssey guide is helping young people find out what they are good at and what God is calling them to (Isaiah 6.8). Our belief is that we have a core vocation and just work it out wherever we are – at school, at work, at church, in our communities. Helping young people see their giftedness and their unique contribution is something which is very precious. One of the tools we use to help with discovering vocation is the examen (see Linn *et al.* 1995 for a youth-friendly version). This can be used to help young people develop self-awareness and discernment about vocation and other aspects of life. The two key questions are:

- Where or when did you find consolation, joy, life or feel alive, recharged, contentment?
- Where or when did you find desolation, death, draining, despair, frustration, sorrow?

Choose whichever period and word you think is most suitable for the young person you are working with. As well as the examen, having some basic tools to help young people reflect and process is useful – formulae such as:

- What? So what? Now what? (Rolfe *et al.* 2001: 35).
- Describe – what do I do? Inform – what does this mean? Confront – how did I come to be like this? Reconstruct – how might I do things differently? (Smyth 1996: 50).

You may not actually use the terms with young people, but they can be helpful frameworks for reflection.

Jenny

Jenny was a challenging client for the school's youth worker. She was a school-refuser who the youth worker was expected to get through to. At first the youth worker wanted to refer her on, feeling out of her depth, but Jenny wouldn't work with anyone else. She was a square peg in a round hole. Eventually Jenny and the youth worker recognized that she was on the autistic spectrum; she was finally diagnosed with Asperger's syndrome and was able to access appropriate education, which resulted in her going to university. Jenny may not have got to where she wanted in the usual way, but she got there in her own way.

Sometimes we will be called to think outside the box when accompanying young people. We will have to push past fixed and firm views of the paths that we think should be taken and find the right path for that young person.

It can be helpful to have some criteria to help make decisions and reflect on advice, insight and revelation, such as:

1 Is it in harmony with our understanding of the Bible?
2 Is it coherent with our values?
3 Does it build the kingdom of God?
4 Do I have an inner peace beyond 'If it feels good, do it!'?
5 Do I sense the witness of the Holy Spirit?
6 Can I do this with integrity?
7 Is it in line with my personal and/or professional ethics?
8 Am I willing to be accountable over this?
9 Have I discussed this with others or brought it to my community? Why? Why not?   (Nash and Nash 2009: 6)

We can encourage young people to develop their own criteria based on their own values.

Good practice

We need to be aware of good practice as youth workers. Others need to feel safe with us, which means that we need to be aware of the dynamics of the relationship, the boundaries that are important. We will normally need to stay in our role. This does not mean that we are being inauthentic. We need to be who we are, we need to be willing to share, to open our lives to others, but in such a way that they are encouraged or empowered or educated rather than wanting to escape because they no longer have that sense of safety or security with us. Also, if young people are to become autonomous in the truest sense, then we need to know when to let go so that they can begin to discover their own unique mission and purpose, thus further shaping their individual identity.

Journeying with ourselves

If we are to be effective odyssey guides we need to be aware of our own journey. Each of us has been on a journey and has arrived at the place where we are now. For some it will have been hard work, depending on what social and emotional circumstances have created along the way, but it is clear that life and all its wonders will present challenges that call us to change. Challenges faced can include so many different things, for example:

- taking on too much personal responsibility for things outside our control or for other people;
- trying to get other people to see the world as we see it rather than celebrating the way that they see it;
- feeling that we are lost or far away from God when he promises to never leave us;
- allowing fear to overtake us rather than trusting in God;
- forgetting we are human and are allowed to fail or have a bad day;
- feeling lonely and isolated because of our lack of self-worth or willingness to accept the love offered by others;
- putting up walls or barriers to others because of all the hurt we have experienced.

We will be on our own journey towards wholeness as we encourage young people in theirs.

One of the key areas to grow as a youth worker is in the area of emotional intelligence. Goleman (1999) promotes the idea of emotional education which encompasses the development of emotional literacy and emotional intelligence. This includes the capacity for recognizing our own feelings and those of others, for motivating ourselves, and for managing emotions well in relationships and in ourselves. He goes on to say that a lack of emotional literacy affects intellectual performance, communication and social skills, arguing that, at most, IQ contributes about 20 per cent to the factors that determine life success, leaving 80 per cent to such factors as emotional intelligence or EQ.

Being emotionally intelligent encourages self-reflection and calls us towards continual personal and professional development. It encourages us to ask ourselves a question without self-criticism, 'Are we part of the problem or part of the solution?' And if we are emotionally intelligent we will be able to answer honestly. Being congruent and having integrity ensures we live by a set of principles that are immovable, leading us towards the goal of saying and doing what we believe in. The reward is that we develop stronger, more trusting and authentic relationships. We model honesty and vulnerability, reducing the risk of others putting us on false pedestals.

Journeying does have possibilities for growth and enlightenment, helping us fulfil our potential in God, becoming more Christ-like, better able to fulfil our vocation and help others on their journey. However, this is not always our experience. There are many reasons for this, such as a lack of self-awareness or knowledge, a fear of what might happen, or the reaction or discouragement of others, particularly those close to us. We may get frustrated as we visit or revisit these things but, as Vanzant writes:

> Trials are but lessons that you have failed to learn, presented once again, so that where you made faulty choices before you can now make a better one, and thus escape all pain that what you chose before has brought you. In every difficulty, all distress, and each perplexity, Christ calls to you gently and says, 'My child, choose again.'   (1999: 128)

But in journeying we find out who we are, as people made in the image of God (Genesis 1.27), with a calling and purpose (Ephesians 2.10) and task (Matthew 28. 16–20): this is a lifelong process.

Conclusion

Being an odyssey guide is often an integral part of being a youth worker; it involves being alongside young people and accompanying them on their journey; it is about being there as much as, if not more than, doing something. Most of us will have a variety of people in our lives who have acted as guides, who have helped us to find our way, to discover who we are and overcome some of the challenges of the journey. We may not be able to be with a young person for the full length of the journey, but the time that we do have can be valuable and genuinely make a difference. However, to be an effective odyssey guide we need to be on a journey ourselves, a journey that will sometimes mean we have to go back in order to go forward. It is a journey that should enable us to capture the gift of our humanity. It is one we were never made to make alone.

Questions for reflection

- What significant things have shaped and changed your life's journey?

- List the people who have been significant odyssey guides in your own life. What characteristics or values did they have that impressed you?
- Try writing your own mission or purpose statement for your own life, including your dreams, ambitions and passions.
- What are your own qualities and strengths as an odyssey guide?

References and further reading

Erikson, E. H., 1995. *Childhood and Society*. London, Vintage.

Freire, P., 2005. *Teachers as Cultural Workers*. Cambridge, MA, Westview Press.

Goleman, D., 1999. *Developing Emotional Intelligence*. New York, Bantam. Helpful guide to how we can become more emotionally intelligent.

Knight, G and Knight, J., 2010. *Called by Mind and Spirit*. London, Continuum. Explores vocation and development from a Christian perspective.

Langford, J., 2006. *Can We Have a Chat?* Cambridge, Grove. Excellent introduction to one-to-one work.

Lefevre, M., 2010. *Communicating with Children and Young People and Making a Difference*. Bristol, Policy Press. Social work practice book with lots of helpful material.

Linn, D., Linn, S. F. and Linn, M., 1995. *Sleeping with Bread*. Mahwah, NJ, Paulist Press. Accessible picture book based on the examen.

Monbourquette, J., 2003. *How to Discover your Personal Mission*. London, Darton, Longman and Todd.

Nash, S. and Nash P., 2009. *Tools for Reflective Ministry*. London, SPCK. Lots of ways to help people reflect theologically.

Rolfe, G., Freshwater, D. and Jasper, M., 2001. *Critical Reflection for Nursing and the Helping Professions*. Basingstoke, Palgrave.

Smyth, J., 1996. 'Developing socially critical educators', in, D. Boud and N. Miller (eds) *Working with Experience*. London, Routledge.

Taylor, A., 2003. *Responding to Adolescents*. Lyme Regis, Russell House. Full of practical help in journeying with young people.

Taylor, D., 1996. *The Healing Power of Stories*. Dublin, Gill and Macmillan.

Vanzant, I., 1999. *Yesterday I Cried*. London, Simon and Schuster.

Vygotsky, L. S., 1978. *Mind in Society*. Boston, Harvard University Press.

11

Compassionate presence

ROBIN BARDEN

The purpose of human life is to serve and to show compassion and
the will to help others.   (Albert Schweitzer)

Introduction

As a metaphor within the practice of Christian pastoral care, 'a compassionate presence' feels an easy concept to grasp but a difficult one
to put into practice or 'be'. While this difficulty often comes from the
simple question of 'what does compassion actually look like in this
specific situation?' it is often complicated further by the plethora of
techniques that come down to us from various quarters, not least
from the field of counselling and from the variety of tools at our
disposal for communication and engagement, such as web-based
social networking. However, these techniques and tools are best learnt
on the job, from those experienced in their specific use, and as with
apprenticeship models of medieval guilds their wise use is best gained
through working alongside such master craftsmen. It is for this
reason, and the restrictions of a chapter such as this to do justice to
the range of tools and techniques that may be needed in any given

situation, that I will be focusing not on skills and techniques themselves but on the wisdom that is essential in their application. This is not to downplay the need to learn skills and techniques but to suggest that you engage with specific literature as and when you need to and seek to learn from relevant master craftsmen as they go about their trade. I will be grappling with the crucial role of compassion in guiding and directing the use of these techniques and tools.

The Good Samaritan and compassion

Nolland (1993: 593) explores how 'the story climaxes with the mention of the Samaritan's compassion', identifying that 'when we come to εσπλαγχνιοη, "he had compassion", we reach the fulcrum upon which the story turns'. All too often we interpret the parable in order to determine what the Priest and Levite *didn't do* and why they didn't do it. But of course the parable itself doesn't address this question as such, and accordingly it seems that as far as the point of the parable is concerned, it is not of primary relevance. The principal point of the parable is, as indicated above, that the Samaritan *had* compassion and that this compassion marked the Samaritan's behaviour out in such a way that the scribe Jesus was originally talking to (and whom we need to remember had some grasp of God and his kingdom – see Luke 10.25–28) understood it to be the actions of a person living in right relationship with God: someone who had inherited eternal life; someone living in the light of and within the rule of God that Jesus had come to establish on earth once and for all: a true Israelite, a kingdom person (Wright 1997). The Samaritan is *thus* seen to be good: holy, of God, righteous.

Compassion as an emotion

Interpreting the parable thus has brought us to the following insight: at the heart of holiness, what N. T. Wright among others calls 'the praxis of the kingdom' (1997: 218; the kingdom as newly inaugurated by Jesus, that is), is an *emotion*. And within Western cultures in the twenty-first century, perhaps especially in the United Kingdom and North America, basing behaviour on emotion is highly problematic. However, that we find it problematic is not a reason to ignore the thrust of the parable or, worse, to rewrite it in light of a twenty-first century ethical concern for universal benevolence, human rights and equality (Nolland 1993: 597). The embodied response of the Samaritan was to a specific situation and crucially, therefore, it was a *felt* response that arose from out of that situation as the Samaritan stumbled into it (Taylor 2007).

To reduce the Samaritan's compassion to a learnt 'ought' in a pre-imagined situation (i.e. to think that the Samaritan was godly because he knew beforehand to always help anyone left half-dead at the side of the road and in the moment of decision dismissed all other messages, including – and especially – any feelings telling him to act differently) is to make the potentially fatal mistake of reducing compassion to a set of predetermined behaviours disconnected from how one feels in the situation, and therefore from the situation itself and the people within it: a road that leads away from 'being' compassionate as a *compassionate presence*, towards acting correctly in the name of a pre-constructed concept. To ignore emotion in this way is not only to dismiss a part of who we are and in doing so play fast and loose with how we actually make decisions, but also to cause a separation of emotion and reason that has arguably been at the root of much abuse in the Christian community and the worst atrocities in twentieth-century society (Jacobs 2000). However, to go the other way and reduce the Samaritan's response to a feeling which allows free reign to the individual in a form of 'moral subjectivity' – I feel, therefore it is right – is also a mistake. Twenty-plus years of experience in Christian ministry have unfortunately provided me with far too many examples of when great harm has been done by well-meaning and/or immature Christians because they believed and felt what they were doing was right, even when the advice they received told them otherwise.

Were the Priest and Levite simply uncaring?

One of the reasons we as Christians may fall into one or both of these errors is because we see the parable as obvious: the Samaritan *just knew* it was right to help, and both the Priest and Levite were simply uncaring and/or following the wrong code. But in fact we do not know what the Priest and Levite felt as they stumbled across the wounded Jew; we certainly cannot assume that they didn't feel *any* compassion (Kilgallen 2008). We do know, however – and must address – that what they felt was qualitatively different from what the Samaritan felt: if the Priest and Levite did feel compassion towards the wounded Jew then how they felt this was different from how the Samaritan felt compassion within the same situation – this is the point of the parable! Of course, the Priest and Levite may simply have felt nothing but disdain – abhorrence, even – nothing! But if we are to give them more credit as human beings – I have met very few people who feel nothing when faced with another human in distress and I have worked in a maximum security prison with people who have committed horrendous and unspeakable crimes – then, at best, they felt a mix of emotions which, while including compassion, also involved contrary emotions. And such contrary emotions may well have been informed by the way their understanding of holiness or the 'good life' framed the situation; accordingly, this may well have included feelings of disdain but not to the same degree – and their feelings may also have been informed by primary impulses such as the fear of being killed oneself. The point is that in our best-case scenario, a scenario that resonates with my experiences, the problem was that they experienced the situation in such a confused manner that they were not clear how to act. On the contrary, the call to compassion was felt by the Samaritan with enough clarity that he could name the feeling as compassion.

But to repeat the point I made above and as the actions of the Priest and Levite demonstrate, this is not to say that responding to how we feel is adequate in and of itself: there was a difference in how the Samaritan and the Priest/Levite *felt*, and while this is central to the parable, and therefore crucial to the insight it brings, it is of equal importance that the Samaritan was ready to respond to the feeling of compassion. The Samaritan stumbled across a situation, felt compassion with enough clarity to name it as such and made the decision to act according to this feeling. For this he was called good, of God. To explore why this was so we must place the parable in its context, both the context in which the parable was told and the context in which Luke places it in the Gospel narrative.

The context in which the parable was told

In the first instance let us consider the broader context. Following N. T. Wright, the parable can be seen within the context of Jesus' proclamation that through and in him the Israelites had returned from exile, that God's rule had been established and that the boundaries of this kingdom encompassed the whole of creation – which importantly means that all nationalities and races, including Samaritans, are now incorporated into the kingdom along with Israel! And, of course, within this grand narrative, Jesus' death and resurrection is the fulcrum upon which it and therefore all eternity turns: it is through and in the death and resurrection of Jesus Christ that we are incorporated into God's kingdom and therefore called to be kingdom people. It is through and in Jesus' death and resurrection that we have communion with God as his children/subjects, receiving or entering into a profound fellowship with God the Holy Spirit: the guide into all truth (John 15.13). The Holy Spirit facilitates our transformation into kingdom people who, reflecting our ruler, are marked by the nature of God: the praxis of *agapé* love. The parable of the Good Samaritan proclaims that God's kingdom, as newly inaugurated through and in Jesus, is open to everyone precisely because it was a non-Jew, a Samaritan, and not the Priest or Levite, who in being compassionate demonstrated not only that he knew God, but that he had allowed this communion with God to transform his view of the 'good life' so profoundly that he felt the call of compassion from the half-dead Jew lying in the ditch with powerful clarity, and knew this feeling to be of God (Wright 1997). There is no subjective 'I decide' here; there is God's kingdom and God's rule only.

This insight also helps to make sense of both the immediate context of the parable as an answer to one half of an irreducible command: 'You shall love the Lord your God with all your heart, and with all your soul, and with all your strength, and with all your mind; *and your neighbour as yourself*' (Luke 10.27, italics mine), and the pairing of the parable with the story of Martha and Mary. The point is that love of neighbour and love of God cannot be separated precisely because each leads into the other, much like a dance. We are perhaps most familiar with the idea that love of God will lead into love of others, but the point now made is that in our desire to love others, as wholeheartedly as God's subjects are called to do, we are inevitably driven to love of God, precisely because, if we are honest with ourselves, we are confronted by our own lack of love, our ungodliness (Nolland 1993).

The skills section

It is important to note that the work of the Holy Spirit is not magical; it is the work of transformation through communion with the God of Love. It is the impact of seeing God that transforms us into those who, like the Good Samaritan, allow right feelings of compassion to direct and guide our pastoral responses. But this is a work that has its own set of skills to master.

Self-awareness

Self-awareness is vital for all youth ministry, but in pastoral care it is particularly important because of the capacity to harm others. For example, try practising tuning yourself into your feelings as they arise in order to recognize where there is confusion and where you may need to ask for help. You may also want to explore whether this confusion is not simply because you are unsure what to do or because you are confused about the vision of the kingdom that God is calling you to and the vision you want young people to pursue. This vision emerges out of worship, discussion and reflection on the story of God within the community of God and therefore requires that over time we place ourselves within and beneath this truth (Hauerwas and Willimon 1989).

Humility

Humbly accept that the journey into both an understanding of and full-hearted commitment to God's kingdom is your lifetime's work. Accordingly, while it brings the insight that as sinners we do not feel or see God's will clearly, it is both our prayer and our motivation to know more fully the fullness with which we are known by God so that we may better feel and see what is the compassionate, merciful response in any given situation.

Communing with God

We believe that Scripture has the authority to show us God through Jesus Christ and so it is to Scripture that we turn. However, as N. T. Wright (2005) explores in his small but insightful book *The Last Word*, to come under the authority of Scripture is not as simple as it may sound, involving as it does engagement with tradition and reason, while ensuring:

- a totally contextual reading of Scripture, which involves valuing the different and changing experiences of various readers, including yourself!
- a liturgically grounded reading of Scripture, which values Scripture incorporated within corporate worship;
- privately studied reading of Scripture, allowing for the kind of personal engagement that often results in authentic, humble prayer;
- a reading of Scripture refreshed by appropriate scholarship: not to undermine faith but to recognize that all churches are part of a larger community, journeying together with gifts spread across the whole body, and that no one has an exclusive right to God;
- a reading of Scripture taught by the churches' accredited leaders: again, this is not to allow abuses such as heavy shepherding but a call to choose leaders wisely.

I only have the space here to flag up the complex nature of coming under the authority of Scripture and I therefore encourage you to read *The Last Word* for yourself.

Being accountable

Policy and procedures, good practice and being accountable are essential tools in ensuring that in our ignorance we do not work against the kingdom and the best interests of the young person. Partnership working and referral are marks not of failure but of a dedication to true compassion. Team working is a must. Your church or agency are likely to have guidelines on pastoral care and certainly should have a safeguarding or child protection policy; make sure you are aware what they are and how you comply with them. Jon Langford's booklet (Grove Booklets 2010) offers wisdom on working with young people one-to-one.

Articulating emotions

Learn how to remain with and tease out feelings of compassion, no matter how diminished or confused they may appear at the time. With others, in light of the stages above, work hard to imagine what compassion looks like within the situation in question and act accordingly.

Common sense

Compare what you consider to be compassionate against the wisdom of others. True compassion seeks the best for people and therefore desires to learn what is truly best for others; as such, it is willing to challenge long-held beliefs and explore new information as it arises, from wherever it arises. Diligently and painstakingly, it explores all relevant information including the observable consequences of actions. As with the scribe's response in the parable of the Good Samaritan, it is often just obvious by using common sense to discern what the loving or neighbourly or kingdom response is. Tough love, so-called, is *always* the exception to the rule, not the guiding principle: the guiding principle is always compassion and mercy – ultimately it is always most hesitant of doing something which could cause harm to another.

True compassion comes from the heart of God and therefore readily acknowledges, in all humility, our own limitations; and while always looking to overcome these it is, at the same time, in light of the previous point, most painfully aware that to deny these limitations is to risk harming others in a way that true compassion finds unacceptable. As such, talking, learning and drawing on the strengths of others are considered a great blessing, *as is the safety of working within good-practice guidelines.* Prayer, rather than naive action, is its first port of call (it is perhaps no accident that Luke places Jesus' teaching on prayer – the 'Our Father' – immediately after the couplet of parables we have been discussing, i.e. the Good Samaritan and Martha and Mary).

True compassion is of the kingdom, and therefore we have faith that God the Father, through Jesus Christ and in the power of the Holy Spirit, will transform us more and more each day into truly compassionate people. Accordingly, we live in the hope that as we stumble upon situations we will begin to feel correctly and act according to God's will, bringing God's kingdom to fruition in our here and now.

Using tools wisely

As with the Samaritan we can only draw on the tools we have at hand – money, time and talents, yes, but also methodologies, resources and experience. But while some tools have been used by Christians in a variety of traditions over substantial periods of time other tools, such as social networking sites, are much more recent additions to our tool box. Accordingly, wisdom in the best use of the former is greater, more widely tested and more readily available than wisdom in the use of the latter. However, this should not deter us from engaging with this wisdom but rather should prompt us to search it out with greater diligence precisely because it is less likely to be in the ether, as it were. As a good place to start I would recommend Nicola David's Grove booklet listed in the References at the end of this chapter, as well as articles in relevant magazines such as *Youthwork* ('Saving face', November 2010) and recognized websites such as <www. childnet-int.org>. Tools mentioned in other chapters of this book may also be of use.

Conclusion

Trusting in emotion to guide our responses is inherently dangerous. It is for this reason that I am passionate about developing self-awareness, engagement with Scripture and dialogue with the wisdom of others. However, we must all start somewhere and therefore it is essential that we look to those around us who are more experienced to guide us in the first instance, as well as the various texts on relevant subjects: I would recommend the Grove booklet series as a good place to start.

Listening to others, being careful with 'oughts' and 'shouldn'ts' – these are basic principles, rarely broken. Appreciating that God and his wisdom are found in strange places – you are not the only person who can communicate truth in who and how you are as well as what you say – guards against pride and its child, coldness.

To be a true compassionate presence comes ultimately from a lifetime's walk with God, but it *is* what comes from this walk.

Questions for reflection

- How do you understand compassion and mercy?
- Are you driven to know God more so that you can be more compassionate?
- Are you willing to listen to others and take their advice regarding how best to help others?

- Do you appreciate the inherent godliness of good-practice guidelines?
- Do you believe that God's kingdom people are marked by the praxis of love?
- Are you called to be a compassionate presence among young people?

References and further reading

Griffiths, S., 2010. *God of the Valley*. Oxford, BRF. A personal, biblically rooted story of a grief journey.

Grove Booklets – accessible introductions to a variety of topics including *Can We Have a Chat? Working safely with young people one to one* by Jon Langford (2010); *Self-esteem and Young People* by Liz Etherton (2008); *Staying Safe Online* by Nicola David (2007); *Wellbeing and Spirituality* by Sally Nash and Nigel Pimlott (2010). See <www.grovebooks.co.uk> to order.

Hauerwas, S. and Willimon, W. H., 1989. *Resident Aliens: Life in the Christian colony*. Nashville, Abingdon Press.

Jacobs, A., 2000. 'George Elliot: good without God', in *First Things*, at <www.leaderu.com/ftissues/ft0004/reviews/jacobs.html>.

Kilgallen, J. J., 2008. *20 Parables of Jesus in the Gospel of Luke*. Chicago, Loyola Press.

Nolland, J., 1993. 'Luke 9:21–18:34', in *Word Biblical Commentary*, Vol. 35b. London, Thomas Nelson.

Pattison, S., 2000. *A Critique of Pastoral Care*. London, SCM. For those who want to explore the concept more deeply.

Taylor, C. A., 2007. *Secular Age*. London, Harvard University Press.

Wright, N. T., 1997. *Jesus and the Victory of God: Christian origins and the question of God*, Vol. 2. London, Augsburg Fortress Publishers.

Wright, N. T., 2005. *The Last Word: Scripture and the authority of God – getting beyond the Bible wars*. London, HarperOne. Explores the role of the Bible as an authority in our lives.

12

Well-watered tree

IAIN HOSKINS

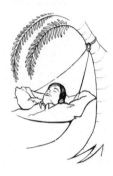

Happy are those
who do not follow the advice of the wicked,
or take the path that sinners tread,
or sit in the seat of scoffers;
but their delight is in the law of the LORD,
and on his law they meditate day and night.
They are like trees planted by streams of water,
which yield their fruit in its season,
and their leaves do not wither.
In all that they do, they prosper.

(Psalm 1.1–3)

Henri Nouwen (2007), talking of the heart of the beloved, challenges us to consider whether we love ourselves. Not in a romantic way, but in a more simple way of looking out for ourselves. When did you last take time to do something which gives you personal pleasure? When did you strike out days in your diary to 'be away'? Not on holiday, but away with God, sitting with your feet in the brook waiting to be restored, revived and reminded that you are not God but one of his servants. For years I worked 24/7, believing that this is what ministry demanded.

No one told me that there was only one end to this type of ministry. When I hit the wall, there was no one there to say what I should do. My wife and I had to work it out with God, who often seemed distant. With not a little nervousness I took a Tuesday off, and the world did not stop; indeed, did anyone notice? When I next suggested a meeting on a Tuesday those I worked with refused, saying, 'It's your day off', and the community became my allies. One of the weaknesses of Christian ministry is that those called can feel as if they have had laid upon them, by others, the responsibility of the world. As youth workers we can be happy to take it on, because it makes us feel valued and wanted.

There was a time, and maybe it still exists in some places, when youth workers believed they were to work all hours of the day, reminding me of Jethro, the father-in-law of Moses. He asked Moses why he worked the way he did and Moses said, 'Because the people come to me' (Exodus 18.15). Jethro helped Moses successfully sort out that problem of overwork.

One youth minister asked his pastor, 'How many hours do I need to work each week?'

'No less than any of the volunteers who work during the day and then come and serve in the evenings or at weekends,' was the reply.

It can feel as though the job is never finished. The youth worker can be like Sisyphus in Greek mythology, whose fate it was to push a great stone up a mountain only to have it roll down again just before reaching the top. This worker left the church, taking up employment with the local authority, where he declared he had never seen such a level of support and concern for a worker's well-being, although I know of people who will say the converse too.

Historical context

Within Martin Luther's (1483–1546) reformed church, care took the form of the application of the Word of God to the needs of the people. Martin Bucer (converted through John Calvin in 1518) argued that the Church should be characterized by close and deep fellowship of both a spiritual and material nature. The Wesleyan (1703–91) tradition was for the pastor to have authority exercised in a persuasively and gentle manner, guiding the flock in all ways of truth and holiness. Nineteenth-century preachers like Charles Haddon Spurgeon believed ministry to be essentially preaching, but also believed that the effectiveness of the preacher was found in his having shared the agony of others (a belief shared by Nouwen 1994). However, none of these preachers had a system or technique as the basis from which care was to be delivered. Today, much has been written about pastoral care (e.g. Goodliff 1998; Graham 2002; Litchfield 2006; Noddings 2003; Pattison 2000); depending on our perspective, it is likely that we will find an author with whom we resonate, but as carers we need to be able to effectively care for ourselves.

Introducing self-care

While talking to the worker I was being distracted by the flashes of vibrant pink fingernails. After a few moments I stopped and asked, 'Are they your fingernails?'

'No, they are acrylic, stuck on with glue, and I love them! My friend Tilley does it, and every two weeks I get them maintained because they get chipped.' The next week I noticed they had changed shape and style but were still immaculate.

Valuing ourselves is very important. God valued Elijah. After his engagement with King Ahab, God sent him off to the Kerith Ravine, east of the Jordan. 'You will drink from the brook, and I have ordered the ravens to feed you there' (1 Kings 17.4, NIV). God's care is always very practical and often involves something that we like doing, or is good for us, like a massage, a trip to a spa, a football match, a game of golf or just watching the television.

Care is an individual and corporate activity. While Tilley cares for the worker's nails she is doing more than a job: she is allowing the worker time to stop, be rested, restored, reflect and feel spoilt and not to feel guilty about giving herself some time. Care forms the basis of Christians' understanding of how to love one another, with God giving us models of practice. As we explore the 23rd Psalm we see the care that God has for us, 'Even though I walk through the darkest valley, I fear no evil; for you are with me; your rod and your staff – they comfort me.' Care is love, best when we receive it with open hands and grateful heart.

Caring for the carers – a dilemma

During conversations one glorious summer day in Reading, youth workers talked about their ability to give care but the immense difficulty in receiving it. Why should this be when Campbell says 'pastoral care is, in essence, surprisingly simple, its aim is to help people to know love, both as something to receive and something to give' (1985: 1)? Sometimes we are very willing to give but don't expect to receive. One youth minister after giving out the notices for the coming week told the young people, 'I will pray for you during the coming week.' As the leader was standing at the door saying goodbye to the young people one 13-year-old asked, 'What can I pray for you in this next week?' The leader was dumbstruck; after a mumbled response the young person left, but the worker was left with a greater question about how a worker responds to this type of care. One dilemma identified by Graham (2002) and Noddings (2003) is that historically pastoral care has been male-dominated, which means that solutions are perceived as tasks to be completed rather than answers worked out through relationships. If self-care is seen as just another task on a list to be ticked off then it may well not be the genuine sort of care we need.

As a worker, employed or voluntary, the 'one-caring' is also in a relationship of being the 'cared-for' (Noddings 2003), and it is in this relationship that workers feel unsettled. Workers can express their feelings for the 'cared-for' when they are in the 'one-caring' role but sometimes they have difficulty when it comes to being the 'cared-for' themselves. This is evidenced when a worker is unwell and away from work. The normally 'one-caring' often rejects offers of care from the 'one-caring' (his or her manager) because he or she feels that to do so will show vulnerability that may be exploited by the 'one-caring' (manager) at a future stage. The result of this situation is that workers may toil on when they know they should stop, and as a result the quality of work overall deteriorates. They are unable to care for themselves properly by accepting the care of others.

Leaders need to recognize their role and try to engage in a reassessment of their understanding of care and their ethics of care. Within this re-evaluation is the recognition of reciprocity in caring relationships, give and take. The assumption of a youth worker in a caring relationship can be that 'my caring is complete if the other feels cared for'. The ethic that needs to be developed is one of reciprocity, where youth workers and young people can, for example, support and pray for one another without the worker or young person feeling weakened because they are sharing a personal need (with workers being aware of appropriate boundaries in what they share).

God and the Church

I believe that one of the reasons that a youth worker may find it hard as the one caring to receive care has its roots in the worker's relationship with God. A former colleague of mine said the Church has domesticated God. If this is the case then we have taken away some of the essentials of God's nature, and since Christians are made in the image of God then those who follow him are a version of the God we have been presented with rather than the real thing. The integrity of our ministry is partly dependent upon how we as youth workers present ourselves, in relationship with God and his Church and the ministry we are called to exercise. When God called us into ministry he called us, not another person's interpretation of us or our own distorted perception of ourselves. Understanding in depth the God in whose image we are created can help us be the person God called us to be, free to care and be cared for.

Only when we recognize God's love and return it is love circulated and complete. Unrecognized and un-responded to, it is love crippled and frustrated. The channel through which we learn about God and intimacy, in principle, is the Church. Yet ironically not all churches have grasped the idea of intimacy and biblical truth. Without the living and challenging God at the very centre of our faith we cannot begin to understand the meaning of love or how love relates to the rest of our lives today. The routes to intimacy with God are not as hard as we make out. As we live in this 'must' and 'ought' world, we need to find the courage to step out from the shadow of those around us and discover who we are.

Sharing as self-care

One of the most effective ways of caring for ourselves is to ensure that we have someone with whom we can share the ups and downs of our ministry (whether we volunteer or are paid). Some call this non-managerial supervision; others may use a spiritual director, soul friend or mentor. Through listening to and trusting one another we will encourage each other often to do things that on our own we might not have done. Those who are willing to trust others and are willing to come out from behind their mask of dedication, timidity or sheer 'I can't', and dare to surrender to themselves as part of a greater whole, will see personal and practical benefits. This can often be achieved through non-managerial supervision, where workers meeting with a trusted other have the opportunity to have:

- space to meet regularly and talk through the issues arising from the course of their work;
- space to step back from the coal face and reflect on their practice;
- space to develop sound strategies for future work.

It is through this non-managerial supervision process, modelled by Jesus with the disciples and Jesus with his Father, that the disciples and workers are able to:

- provide support to one another;
- identify and pursue development needs;
- provide a context in which work and workload are monitored.

All workers need to regularly review their practice by identifying the issues that are affecting their work in advance of a meeting, and to be prepared to share freely within the group or meeting space. Ask yourself, 'What is it I would like to take away from this meeting?', being aware of organizational limitations (see Helm and Allin 2002).

Feedback as self-care

One feature that is often lacking in people is that of being open to constructive feedback. If we are to learn from one another and from ourselves then we need to hear constructive criticism and learn from it, recognizing that sometimes we tend to justify, explain and defend. Nouwen says, 'People are *called*, and when they follow the gentle urging of the voice that calls them they are led, despite everything to the contrary, to a place of green pastures' (Beumer 1997: 92). Listening to and responding to the voice of God is what protects us all from the loss of confidence and faith in what we are doing and builds our relationships with other team members. Often the voice of God is heard through others.

Making space as self-care

Even when we know what we need – space, restoration and peace – we simply go along with the many 'musts' and 'oughts' that have been handed on to us. We live with them as if they were authentic translations of the gospel of our Lord. If we are to be men and women of God then we need to take responsibility for ourselves in every dimension: no one will do it for us. Paul Borthwick calls this process *Feeding the Forgotten Soul*; Christopher Jamison, former Abbot of Worth Abbey, calls it *Finding Sanctuary*; Elaine Storkey goes *In Search of Intimacy* and those of the Celtic traditions look for a sacred space.

Finding sanctuary will enable busy youth workers to find ways of listening to God and self within the demanding world in which we live. There will be opportunities for listening to each other, building our own sanctuary and discovering how we can share our peace with others. As free people we can choose how busy we want to be. Freely choosing to resist the urge to busy-ness is the frame of mind you need before you can take any steps towards finding sanctuary. As well as tourism, other industries are springing up around the 'too busy' belief: health spas called 'Sanctuary', offering 'heaven'; radio stations called 'Smooth', offering relaxation and 'alternative therapies' that eliminate all stress.

Can real understanding be reached without a deep respect for that holy place within and between us, that space that should remain untouched by human hands? Can human intimacy really be fulfilling when every space within and between us is being filled up? Nouwen talks about the need to break through our fear to express our true feelings and be able to be open and honest with others, to find someone who cares: this, then, would bring inner peace (1978).

St Benedict, founder of the order of St Benedict and Western monasticism, knew that he could spend too much time on the wrong things. Above all, as youth ministers we must not show great concern for the fleeting and temporal things of this world, while neglecting or treating lightly upon the welfare of those entrusted to us. The basic starting point for entering sacred sanctuary is the quality of our day-to-day dealings with other people. Finding the sacred space begins with the recognition of the sacred in our daily living. I always thought this to be a very difficult thing to do: where are those sacred places, what do they look like and when will I know I have arrived? Well, I have found one and I never knew it: the place is my study at home. When I go into work I first light a candle, then offer a prayer of thanksgiving and intercession for the work to be done and all that will happen in that place today. The candle is a visual reminder to me of the ever-present God and his Spirit. As I work away I never feel alone; we chat and reflect upon things and people, and when the day is done I say thank you. The sacred space that eluded me for so long was only a step away once my eyes were open and I could see.

Another of my reservations is silence and being alone; I never liked coming home from school to an empty house. However, I have discovered that I am often alone when driving the motorways, sitting on aeroplanes, sitting in airport lounges waiting for flights. I found that my aloneness is human-made. The task is finding positive silence in your local setting. When entering silence, the first thing you discover is the distractions inside you – what Benedict calls the weeds. The flowers in this case are the words from God that can grow if you have cleared a space for them. The trouble is that the weeds grow faster than the flowers and we give up. The time it takes to create and nurture the space for the flowers to grow is found in silence through solitude, an often short-term activity valued as a time when one may work, think or rest without being disturbed. Henri Nouwen (1996) speaks of solitude as the start of the spiritual life, arguing that a person who has developed this solitude of the heart will no longer be pulled apart by the most divergent stimuli of the surrounding world but is able to perceive and understand this world from a quiet inner centre.

Conclusion

How then does a person involved in busy ministry survive the journey? From what we have seen, the writers are helpful and wise yet not in agreement. There are many ways to peace and we each need to find the way that works for us. The first thing we need to do is to discover who we are, rather than wrestling with the person others would like us to be. We need to find a space where we can be with God, and this does not have to be on a mountain – it could be in a shopping mall. For several years I have led quiet days in the centre of Bristol. The people involved are all generally sceptical at the beginning that they will find God at all. I tell them: be patient, listen, watch and wait upon God; you will meet him in many different ways, and sometimes in the noise of the city you will hear that whisper (1 Kings 19.11–13) speaking to you – as everyone knows, it isn't necessary to talk with someone to know that he or she is with you. Finally, we need to trust in our relationship with God. Do not be anxious: the care we receive will teach us how to care. Pursuing self-care is not selfish: it is what brings us into a place where we can offer appropriate loving, godly care to others.

Questions for reflection

- Are there any barriers that stop you caring for yourself properly?
- What are your favourite self-care activities? How often do you programme them in?
- How easy is it for you to receive care from others? What are the issues for you?
- Who do you have that you can share like this with? Who can you offer such care to?
- When and how do you make space for God? Is there anything more that you could be doing in this area?
- What elements make up your strategy for self-care? Do you need to make any changes in your life or lifestyle?

References and further reading

Beumer, J., 1997. *Henri Nouwen*. New York, Crossroad. Understanding Nouwen helps you to understand his work and then you will begin to see how it is relevant for you.

Borthwick, P., 1993. *Feeding Your Forgotten Soul*. Grand Rapids, MI, Zondervan.

Campbell, A., 1985. *Paid to Care*. London, SPCK.

Goodliff, P., 1998. *Care in a Confused Climate*. London, Darton, Longman and Todd. Care needs to be understood and not seen as an ambulance service. This book will help you to understand how Christians so often get care wrong and what they need to do about it.

Graham, E., 2002. *Transforming Practice*. Eugene, Wipf and Stock. This feminist theologian needs to be read by men who tend to manage care like a mathematical problem. Not the easiest read, but great fun when you drop your prejudices and read for enlightenment.

Helm, N. and Allin, P., 2002. *Finding Support in Ministry*. Cambridge, Grove.

Jamison, C., 2006. *Finding Sanctuary*. Collegeville, MN, Liturgical Press.

Litchfield, K., 2006. *Tend My Flock*. Norwich, Canterbury Press.

Noddings, N., 2003. *Caring*, second edition. California, University of California Press.

Nouwen, H., 1978. 'Celibacy', *Pastoral Psychology* 27(2): 79–90.

Nouwen, H., 1994. *The Wounded Healer*. London, Darton, Longman and Todd.

Nouwen, H., 1996. *Reaching Out*. London, HarperCollins.

Nouwen, H., 2007. *Beloved*. Norwich, Canterbury Press. Solitude, silence, knowing self, light and dark: are these your spiritual comfort zones? If not, read this book; simple but profound.

Pattison, S., 2000. *A Critique of Pastoral Care*. London, SCM Press.

Storkey, E., 1995. *In Search of Intimacy*. London, Hodder and Stoughton. Intimacy needs to be understood, and this book addresses the issue from a practical and theological viewpoint, opening doors, letting light into our world of intimacy; exciting.

Appendix

Youth ministry role preferences and passions indicator

This is not a scientific questionnaire but rather an indicator of your preferences and passions as you carry out your youth work. Try to respond in the light of who you are now, not who you would like to be. Think of preferences as what you do when you have a choice; our choices often reflect our calling.

Step 1 Read all the chapters.
Step 2 Read each statement and, using Table A.1 as a guide, score it using this formula:
    (a) this statement is very like me – 3 points;
    (b) this statement is a bit like me – 1 point;
    (c) this statement isn't like me – 0 points.
Step 3 Add up the total number of points for each chapter, metaphor, role.
Step 4 Rank them from 1 to 12, the role or metaphor with the highest score being your most preferred, the one with the lowest score being your least preferred.
Step 5 Reflect on the implications of this for your personal youth ministry. Does anything encourage you? Surprise you? Help you see yourself in a new light? Help you understand how you feel? Confirm what others have said to you? . . .
Step 6 If you are part of a team, encourage others to do this exercise too and then map your team against the roles. Reflect on the implications of this for your youth ministry team.
    Where are you strongest as a team? Where are you weakest? Are there any roles missing? Do you need to adapt or develop your youth work in the light of this reflection?

Table A.1 Youth ministry role preferences and passions indicator

Metaphor/role	Statements	Score	Total	Ranking
Politician of integrity	I am a person of integrity			
	I am aware of the wider dynamics at church			

Metaphor/role	Statements	Score	Total	Ranking
	I am diplomatic and enjoy resolving situations			
	I seek to cultivate virtues in my life			
	Ethics are important to me			
Flawed hero	I enjoy being a role model for young people			
	I find that others look to me to lead			
	I like to point others to Jesus through my words and actions			
	I believe it is important to model good and safe practice			
	I am aware of my weaknesses and seek to be honest about them			
Visionary architect	I am good at seeing the big picture			
	I enjoy long-term planning			
	I work well with a team to achieve goals			
	I have a clear idea of what sort of youth work I want to do			
	I tend to see a project through to the end			
Community builder	I enjoy bringing people together			
	I like people to feel that they belong			
	I try to pass my beliefs on to young people			
	I have a strong sense of faith identity			
	I have a gift of offering hospitality			
Empowering liberator	I enjoy spending time with people, helping them to explore issues and decisions			
	I believe it is important to empower young people			
	I like helping young people see how the Christian work can work for them			
	I use the Bible as a guide for life and encourage others to do the same			
	I want young people to understand the way that they live life			

Metaphor/role	Statements	Score	Total	Ranking
Party planner	I enjoy helping young people celebrate their achievements			
	I enjoy celebrating key Christian festivals with young people			
	I think it is important for young people to have a good time			
	I believe it is possible for young people to have a good time and be holy			
	I like to help young people plan creative events			
Boundary marker	I believe I have a responsibility to help young people be in a safe environment			
	I think it is OK to challenge unhealthy behaviour or attitudes towards themselves or others			
	I work hard to be both compassionate and fair			
	I believe it is possible to challenge certain behaviour without being judgemental			
	I put the needs of the group before the needs of an individual			
Mediating mirror	I believe it is paramount that young people know how God sees them			
	I think I have a primary responsibility to build positive self-esteem with and in young people			
	I find it easy to praise people sincerely			
	I spend my time positively reinforcing the good things I see in young people			
	I do not find it hard to see the good in young people			
Guardian of souls	I believe that building faith in young people is my primary calling			
	It is important for young people to be able to express their doubts about Christianity			

Metaphor/role	Statements	Score	Total	Ranking
	I believe it is more important to share relationally than to just stand at a distance and tell young people what to do			
	I believe the main role of being a Christian young person is to become more of a follower of Jesus			
	I am very creative in helping young people grow in their faith			
Odyssey guide	I am good at supporting young people through their problems			
	I want to see young people make a successful transition to adulthood			
	I try to create a supportive and safe environment for young people			
	I enjoy listening to young people and being fully present to them			
	I like to help people identify their God-given vocation			
Compassionate presence	I believe the most important gift I can give to young people is to love them			
	My primary response to young people is to be compassionate			
	I find it easy to be kind and gracious to young people and to give them the benefit of the doubt			
	I believe God's overwhelming attitude towards young people is a compassionate one			
	I desire to know God better so I can express more of his compassion			
Well-watered tree	I find it easy to love myself			
	I have a good work–life balance			
	I regularly do nice things because I am worth it			
	I can easily express my personal needs			
	I regularly make space for God in my life			

Index of biblical references

Index of subjects